# Abba, Father

Kenneth Stevenson is the Bishop of Portsmouth and a member of the Doctrine Commission of the Church of England.

A leading Anglican scholar, his many published works include *The Mystery of Baptism*, *The Mystery of the Eucharist in the Anglican Tradition* (co-authored with Henry R. McAdoo) and *All the Company of Heaven*, all by the Canterbury Press, and *Covenant of Grace Renewed* by Darton, Longman and Todd.

# Abba Father

*Understanding and
Using the Lord's Prayer*

Kenneth Stevenson

MOREHOUSE PUBLISHING
HARRISBURG, PENNSYLVANIA

© 2000 by Kenneth Stevenson

Morehouse Publishing
P.O. Box 1321
Harrisburg, PA 17105

*Morehouse Publishing is a division of The Morehouse Group.*

First published in 2000 by Canterbury Press Norwich
(a publishing imprint of Hymns Ancient & Modern Limited, a registered charity)
St. Mary's Works, St. Mary's Plain
Norwich, Norfolk NR3 3BH, U.K.

Cover design by Tom Castanzo.

A Catalog record for this book is available from the Library of Congress.
ISBN 0-8192-1879-0

Printed in Great Britain
00 01 02 03 04 05    5 4 3 2 1

# Contents

# Prologue

This book has been a long time in the making. I suppose it began many years ago when I first became aware of the fact that there was more than one version of the Lord's Prayer, other than the one I learnt from the Prayer Book. I suppose it took a further step when I became conscious of the fact that it can occupy different positions in public worship. And I suppose that it took on yet more life when it dawned on me that there might be a story to tell, not so much about its origins as about the different ways in which it has been used and about ourselves as part of that living tradition of interpretation.

Two years ago I decided to take the Lord's Prayer around the eight deaneries of the Diocese of Portsmouth on a kind of extended roadshow, while the second millennium gave way to the third. The figure of eight began to produce its own momentum; eight deanery clergy groups to discuss eight different interpreters (part three); eight overlapping issues on the use of the Lord's Prayer to explore at a deanery extended Eucharist (part one); together with time, too, to look at each of the eight petitions of the prayer in turn (part two).

And so the deanery visits took place: Havant, Bishop's Waltham, Portsmouth, Petersfield, Gosport, Fareham, East Wight and West Wight. Ian Jagger, our canon missioner, wrote an eight-verse paraphrase on the Lord's Prayer, reproduced in the Appendix, which we sang at each of the Deanery Eucharists. Our discussions were wide-ranging. What on earth is heaven? Why forgive? Isn't daily bread for the poor as well? And John Hillawi, an Iraqi Christian, asked that we don't forget that the prayer is still uttered today in Aramaic – Jesus' own tongue – by many Christians in the Middle East.

Expanding the addresses in the light of these discussions has provided me with the opportunity to introduce more historical and liturgical comment, including some from the rich tradition of Anglican writing on the Lord's Prayer. I have been constantly struck by the fact that the rich resources of this prayer are as unfathomable as the repertoire of human experience before God. The Lord's Prayer was composed in order to be *used*, hence those 'issues' in part one; the Lord's Prayer was composed in order to be *prayed*, hence those meanings in part two; and the Lord's Prayer has therefore been *interpreted*, hence those theological snapshots (no more) of the selected eight (and it was hard indeed to choose them!) in part three, all of them so different in context, and the medium they chose, whether for preaching or writing. This could well make for different ways of using this book. Some may want to take things as they come; others may want to go straight to part two, preferring to taste the prayer in its sequence first; others may wish to use the inter-preters in part three as their opening; while each part relates directly to the others, they can still stand on their own.

There have been many books and articles on the background of the Lord's Prayer, and my debt to scholars of recent decades is obvious; Ernst Lohmeyer, Jean Carmignac, Ingemar Furberg, Christopher Evans, William Barclay, Oscar Cullmann and Tom Wright, as well as Leslie Houlden, Joachim Jeremias and James Barr. The work which follows, which I want to take further in the coming years, has an historical perspective intended to complement these mainly New Testament studies. I have become increasingly convinced of the prayer's autonomy, determined by its uses, public and private; by its meanings, spiritual and material; and by its interpreters, whether they are biblical scholars or preachers. For an age like ours, grappling with questions of personal significance and interdependence that go far beyond what 'modernity' and 'post-modernity' might ever be, the Lord's Prayer emerges as a living text, full of rich gospel metaphors whether of heavenly fatherhood, hallowing the name, the coming of the kingdom, the doing of the will, or the need for bread, forgiveness and protection.

In offering these pages, I should like to thank many people: my colleagues, Mervyn Banting, Christopher Lowson, Peter Hancock, Michael Jordan and Andrew Tremlett, my Chaplain, who has lived assiduously alongside this project from the start; the Rural Deans of the diocese and the Lay Chairs of the Deanery Synods; catalysts from elsewhere, particularly Martin Kitchen, David Ford, Geoffrey Wainwright, David Tustin, Alan Wilkinson, Ann Loades, Geoffrey Rowell and Bryan Spinks; my companion in prayer, the Roman Catholic Bishop of Portsmouth, Crispian Hollis; Jean Maslin and Julie Anderson for providing me with clean copy whenever I needed it; and Sarah and Alexandra for putting up with an often preoccupied mind. For many years before our move to Portsmouth, the late Dom Joseph Warrilow, monk of Quarr Abbey on the Isle of Wight, used to direct me constantly to the Lord's Prayer as my spiritual mentor. All these strands have come together in the pages which follow, and they have become a book which is dedicated to the clergy and people of the diocese, with much affection.

KENNETH STEVENSON
Bishopsgrove
*Petertide 2000*

# The Lord's Prayer

Our Father in heaven,
hallowed be your name,
your kingdom come,
your will be done,
on earth as in heaven.
Give us today our daily bread.
Forgive us our sins
as we forgive those who sin against us.
Lead us not into temptation
but deliver us from evil.
For the kingdom, the power,
and the glory are yours
now and for ever.
Amen.

# PART ONE

## Issues

# I

# Matthew and Luke – Different Versions

On many occasions I have attended international gatherings when those present have been invited to recite the Lord's Prayer in their own tongue at the same time. I can think of the Bible Study Group of which I was a member during the 1998 Lambeth Conference, when a bevy of languages from all over the world met together in what seemed like a common rhythm, offering the words given by Christ to his disciples, as Matthew's Gospel tells us, in a united act of prayer. The same was true a year later, when the Anglo-Nordic-Baltic Theological Conference met in Fareham, at my house. Each morning in my chapel, we recited that prayer, and the languages included were Swedish, Norwegian, Danish, Finnish, Estonian, Latvian and Welsh, in addition to English. It was never for a moment hard to mould them into a common rhythm as we listened to our neighbours; and we learnt now and again what the words were in their language, not just our own. As the days wore on we developed our own pace, turning the prayer into a symphony in its own right.

Many people tell of the same experience when that sort of thing happens. The Lord's Prayer has its own internal rhythms, thanks to its brevity and direction. It is a unique prayer, because it is the only prayer of its kind that we find in the Bible. It can therefore almost claim to have a 'canonical' status, in being fixed. It is not like any of the other prayers that we use, which have been produced in one generation or another. Some prayers were written centuries ago and translated into English at the

Reformation, like the 'Prayer of St Chrysostom', which begins 'Almighty God, who hast given us grace at this time with one accord to make our common supplications unto thee . . .'. This was written in Greek long before the eighth century text which is the earliest known to us. It was translated into English for the Prayer Book by Archbishop Thomas Cranmer (1488–1556) and it has been used ever since, including in contemporary English translation.

There have been different versions of the Lord's Prayer across the centuries. Alongside the official Latin text of the medieval Church there were vernacular translations, like the following, which was in use in England in Anglo-Saxon times:

Fader ure thu the eart on heofonum,
Si thin nama gehalgod.
Tobecume thin rice.
Gewurthe in willa on earthan swa swa on heofonum.
Urne gedaeghwamlican hlaf syle us to daeg.
And forgyf us ure gyltas,
   swa swa we forgyfath urum gyltedum.
And ne gelaed thu us on contnungen
   ac alys us of yfele.

Those words read strangely and perhaps sound like a mixture of English and one of the German or Nordic languages – which is what Anglo-Saxon is, in an earlier form.

Language develops, and the meanings of words change. When I was a boy, I had to use two different versions each week. At primary school, it was the old Scots Reformation version, with 'forgive us our debts, as we forgive our debtors'; whereas at Church, it was the English Prayer Book version, from 1549, where we ask to be forgiven our trespasses. That experience helped me get used to the fact that there was no one single perfect version of the prayer, as if one particular translation came out of heaven, written by a divine typewriter. New translations are necessary from time to time. And each has its own particular strengths and weaknesses. For example, sins are indeed debts that we owe to other people, and have a 'financial' quality, but they are also ways of moving in on other people's territory and treating it as our own, as the word trespass implies. At the moment, in the English-speaking world we are striving to find agreement on a modern translation, which time and experience alone will eventually yield. Meanwhile, many of us fall back on the older version in its lightly revised form '*who* art in heaven', '*on* earth as it is in heaven', and '*those* who trespass against us'. It often provides a kind of halfway house, for the purposes of security, and for very understandable reasons. One way to indicate which version is to be used is to differentiate the introductory 'cue'-words as in the *Common Worship* (2000) Eucharist. There is unlikely to be ever one single perfect translation of this unique prayer. More important than exactly *what* we say is *how* we say it, the spirit in which we say it, and the many different levels of understanding which these words – most of them quite stark and simple in the original Greek text – convey to us and invoke in us.

\* \* \*

Where is the prayer to be found? There are two versions in the New Testament. One appears in Matthew's Gospel in the middle of what has long been called the Sermon on the Mount – Matt. 6:9–13 – and this, with one or two small editorial alterations, the Church adopted in the three principal 'official' languages of ancient Christianity, namely Greek, Syriac and Latin. But there is another and slightly shorter version, almost halfway through Luke's Gospel, when the disciples asked Jesus how they should pray – Luke 11:2–4. People are often puzzled as to exactly why there are these two versions. The early Christian theologian Origen (c.185–c.254), who was keen to recognize the distinctivenesses of each of the Gospel writers, suggested in this particular case that Jesus spoke the prayer on two occasions, which seems unlikely.[1] The differences, however, are not all that great, as the following layout shows:[2]

| *Matthew 6:9–13* | *Luke 11:2–4* |
|---|---|
| Our Father in the heavens | Father |
| may your name be hallowed | may your name be hallowed |
| may your kingdom come | may your kingdom come |
| may your will come to | |
| pass as in heaven also on | |
| earth | |
| Our bread for the morrow | Our bread for the morrow |
| give us today | give us each day |
| And forgive us our debts as | And forgive us our sins for we |
| we also have forgiven our | also forgive everyone indebted |
| debtors | to us |
| and do not lead us | and do not lead us |
| into test | into test |
| but rescue us | |
| from the evil | |
| one (?) | |

Each of these two versions is entirely characteristic of its Gospel writer. Luke only has 'Father' because he often refers to God as Father and no more (Luke 22:42; 23:34, 46). Matthew on the other hand likes to refer to God as 'our', 'my' or 'your' (Matt. 5:16; 6:4, 9; 26:42) Father and often with the adjective 'heavenly', as well as 'balancing' earth and heaven on several occasions (Matt. 6:19–20; 6:25, 28; 16:19; 18:18 and 28:18). Luke does not include 'Your will be done . . .', but the doing of the will is something of a priority in Matthew's Gospel (Matt. 7:21; 12:50; 18:14; 26:42). Nor does Luke give us the petition for deliverance from evil, but Matthew does, also in line with his own priorities, since evil is mentioned twenty-four times, far more frequently than in the other Gospels; more particularly, it is used of the devil in Matthew 13:19 and 38.

A picture is building up of what looks like separate traditions of the Lord's Prayer, possibly produced by two different communities. Some scholars have suggested that Luke is the original because it is shorter, and that Matthew is an expansion on it; others have suggested that Matthew's is the original, and

Luke's is an abbreviation; others maintain that both rely on a common source, which is the most likely conclusion, irrespective of the variants in Matthew and Luke.[3] We do not know the precise details of how early Christians worshipped, so that it is safe to assume that the short Lucan version was used by some congregations, and that the longer – perhaps more Jewish – Matthew version won through. The earliest liturgical text outside the Bible is to be found in the *Didache* (or 'Teaching'), an early Christian Church Order, which was probably put together in Syria towards the end of the first century or the beginning of the second. Interestingly, its version follows Matthew closely but adds the doxology (*Didache* 8.2) – 'for yours is the power and the glory for ever and ever' – because no Jewish prayer would have ended without one. And it is this doxology, with 'kingdom' added before 'power and glory', that appears in late Greek manuscripts of Matthew's Gospel, sometimes even with the 'Amen'. This is an example of the direct influence of liturgical usage on biblical text. The early Christians were *using* the prayer, and imposed that use on the evolving manuscripts of the Gospels. The doxology, as we shall discover later, was not an integral part of the prayer in the West until after the Reformation. And that explains why there is this basic variant over and above the vagaries of translation.

\* \* \*

But where, it might well be asked, did the Lord's Prayer come from? Its sentiments are steeped in Jewish piety. The fatherhood of God has many Old Testament parallels (Isa. 63:16; 1 Chr. 29:10; Ps. 89:27). The name of God is similarly paralleled (2 Sam. 6:2; Jer. 7:11; Lev. 11:45). The prayer for the coming of the kingdom has looser echoes (Pss 46:7 and 121:5); the doing of the will pervades Psalm 119 (vv 27,30,32,33), and daily bread echoes the feeding with daily manna in the wilderness (Exod. 16:15ff; Num. 11:6ff; Deut. 8:3ff). The forgiveness of God is a constant Old Testament theme, although mutual forgiveness – which is also (and emphatically) prayed for here – is less strongly present, except in exhortation (Lev. 19:18). The Old Testament does indeed teach that God protects the faithful (supremely in the 'sacrifice of Isaac' – Gen. 21), and there are parallels in the prayer for deliverance from evil (1 Sam. 12:10).

From these parallels (and others), the Lord's Prayer emerges as a Christian prayer with strong Jewish roots. Many have meditated on its Old Testament background in more general terms. The great seventeenth-century Anglican writer, Lancelot Andrewes (1555–1626), included in his own devotions no fewer than six paraphrases of the Lord's Prayer from the Old Testament of which the first and briefest is as follows:

> Let thy name be called upon of us (Gen. 4:26).
> Be thou our shield and our exceeding great reward
>     (Gen. 15:1).
> What word so ever proceedeth from thee,
> Let it not be in us to speak aught against it, whether good or
>     bad (Num. 24:13).
> Give us bread to eat and raiment to put on (Gen. 28:20).
> And now pardon the iniquity and the unrighteousness of
>     thy servants (Num. 14:19).
> And, O Lord, let us not think anxiously in our hearts all the
>     day long (Deut. 28:32).
> And let not evils take hold of us (Deut. 31:17).[4]

This 'canonical' prayer, very probably originally spoken in Aramaic, Jesus' own tongue, is a prayer that will go on being used, translated and interpreted. The shorter version in Luke's Gospel does not miss out on anything essential. At some stage, the early Christians decided for Matthew and have remained unanimously so ever since. The variants help to point up the individual character of each individual Gospel writer, and point to a diversity in the unity, a diversity in which (one could say) Christ himself exists. The longer, Matthean, version does, however, provide that bit more space for interpretation. In that regard, perhaps the most important rule of thumb is that the words should be allowed to resonate and apply themselves on different levels. A prayer which builds so much on its Jewish ancestry in the first place, and yet which embodies so much of the Christian gospel, as transmitted to us in the particular styles of Matthew and Luke, is also a prayer whose ways of meaning are of far greater significance than the particular translation agreed on at a particular time.

The centuries yet to come will produce their own translations. I was forcibly reminded of exactly that truth when attending the liturgy of the Syrian Orthodox in the Church of the Holy Sepulchre in Jerusalem. The priest stood there chanting the Lord's Prayer in Aramaic, and immediately my mind went back to the hills of Galilee through which I had driven two days before. At the same time I thought of the new worlds into which those words had been born, including the Student Chaplaincy Church in Manchester where I was ministering at the time, as well as the friends and relatives I was to visit in the following year during a sabbatical in North America. The prayer leaps from its biblical origins, and focuses on its largely Matthean foundation, and then is incarnated into new climates, new situations, new contexts, filling the prayerful lives of worshippers with the words that Jesus is supposed to have taught his disciples – and still does today.

# 2

# Matthew and Luke –Different Contexts

If you look in the windows of an estate agent, you are likely to see photographs of houses presented in the most flattering light possible. But often as important as what the house looks like is its location. Is it near shops? How far is it from a doctor's surgery? What is the surrounding landscape – if any – like? All these are questions that cannot be answered by taking in a quick glance at an advertisement. The only way to do so is to look at that surrounding terrain and examine it carefully.

The same can be said of the two versions of the Lord's Prayer which are given in the Gospels of Matthew and Luke. Matthew's, as we have already observed, is slightly longer than Luke's (cf. Matt. 6:9–13 and Luke 11:2–4). And that – as we have suggested – probably explains why it is the version that the Church decided to use at an early stage. So much, then, for these two houses, which resemble each other. But what of their wider context – the surrounding terrain? For all that the prayers resemble each other closely, their contexts could not be more different.

Matthew's surrounding terrain was first called the Sermon on the Mount by Augustine (354–430), preaching in the 390s in Hippo, North Africa. So far from being a separate part of Matthew's Gospel, it is now increasingly regarded by scholars, particularly Graham Stanton, as an integral part of it.[1] Matthew places the Lord's Prayer halfway through it, embedding prayer and discipleship in the teaching of Jesus. This teaching could be summed up by the words 'open' religion versus 'secret' religion. We are being told not to parade our religion in public – a clear rebuke against those who do exactly that (Matt. 6:1). We are not to parade our piety, nor are we to tell everybody what we give (6:2), because that is a way of drawing unnecessary attention to ourselves. We are not to parade like hypocrites (6:5) – people who like to stand in public and show what they are doing. Instead we are to pray in secret (6:6), carefully withdrawing to do so. In this, Jesus is not saying that public worship is wrong, but that prayer is personal, and it is public only in so far as it is a group of people sharing a common purpose, rather than wanting to signal to each other – and to a watching public – in an ostentatious way. When we pray, we are not to heap up empty phrases, and babble away just for the sake of it (6:7). Some of us often do get carried away – in an understandable enthusiasm – and our prayers, including intercessions, can fill up with information rather than with brevity and space. Many commentators on the Lord's Prayer regard it as a model for all prayer, intercession included, and they commend its strange brevity. Perhaps it was this that made St Benedict write the following words in his *Rule*:

> We must know that God regards our purity of heart and tears of compunction, not our many words. Prayer should therefore be short and pure, unless perhaps it is prolonged under the inspiration of divine grace.[2]

It is at this point, and at this point only, that Matthew has Jesus tell us how to pray, in the words which are indeed personal and brief. But it is much more than words. For no sooner has Jesus finished than he exhorts us to forgive others (Matt. 6:14,15), repeating the point by implying that God will only forgive us our sins if we do the same to others. And when we fast, we are not to parade the fact in public, for the life of faith is not about outward and earthly things; it is about treasure in heaven, where our hearts need to be truly, wonderfully and graciously fixed (Matt. 6:19–21).

Such a prayer-centred life means that our whole body is filled with light and not darkness (Matt. 6:22); and it also means that our lives are more likely to be God-centred, rather than mammon-centred (Matt. 6:24). We do not begin the Lord's Prayer by praying for our own material needs – in the form of daily bread. That daily bread is set in the context of an attitude of life that looks upon God as our heavenly Father, whose name is to be hallowed by us, whose kingdom is to come in us, and whose will is to be done in us. Moreover, such a life of faith involves trust – trust that God will provide what we shall eat and drink, and such matters as our clothing (Matt. 6:25). The life of faith means not being anxious about tomorrow, but seeing each day as a gift for which God will give us sufficient blessing (Matt. 6:34). Trustful obedience, however, must go hand in hand with active discipleship – and that is precisely why, to return to the verses immediately following the giving of the Lord's Prayer, Jesus exhorts his disciples to be men and women of mutual forgiveness (Matt. 6:14–15).

How could the petitions of the Lord's Prayer relate to the opening words of the Sermon on the Mount, which orientates the Christian towards a view of life that is turned upside down? The poor in spirit will be rich enough to possess the kingdom of heaven; the mournful will be comforted; the meek will inherit the earth; those who hunger and thirst for righteousness will have their hunger and thirst satisfied; the merciful are the ones who will obtain what they mete out to others; the pure in heart (rather than, perhaps, the worthily active) will see God; the peacemakers will be called children of God; the persecuted will possess the kingdom of heaven; and those who are reviled and are persecuted are blessed, for their reward is in heaven (Matt. 5:1–11).

A similar reversal is to be found in the Lord's Prayer. The Father in heaven is not my private possession, but belongs to us all. His name and nature are not distant and unattainable but can be hallowed, respected, loved and worshipped, even by human beings. His kingdom is not distant and like a pipe dream, but, as the Beatitudes themselves tell us, is attainable now – by the poor in spirit and by the persecuted. His will, therefore, can be done just as much on earth as it is in heaven, because we are being given the measuring sticks with which to grasp just what this will is about. All this means that our daily bread, our staple diet, will be given us by our heavenly Father, as we co-operate with his work in recognizing him as our Father, hallowing his name, living that kingdom, and trying to do that will. Forgiveness can indeed be ours, provided we forgive others – mercy will be ours if we are merciful ourselves. And the testing that this life will bring – primarily in our lack of faith that these Beatitudes are indeed true, and in our temptation to turn away from God altogether – this is real and recognized in this prayer, and in the subsequent teaching of Jesus himself that we are not to be anxious. Deliverance from evil takes many forms; disregarding the poor in spirit, the mournful, the meek, those who hunger and thirst for righteousness, the merciful, the pure in heart, the peacemakers, the persecuted and reviled; as well as those occasions when we want to turn our religion into a public show and nothing else, when we refuse to forgive, when we seek earthly treasures rather than heavenly, and when we prefer darkness and not light. Matthew's prayer is deeply embedded in the Sermon on the Mount.

*    *    *

What, then, of the surrounding terrain for Luke's version of the Lord's Prayer? Well into the Galilee ministry of Jesus, Luke wrestles with the relationship between prayer and action, in a section which Christopher Evans regards as having been assembled from various different sources.[3] If we take the sequence of material as it comes in Luke, the Lord's Prayer therefore stands out with some prominence. But it can still be related to what surrounds it and perhaps more convincingly to what follows it. Jesus prefaces the giving of the Lord's Prayer with three episodes found only in Luke's Gospel. First of all, Jesus sends out the seventy (Luke 10:1ff), confident that the harvest is plentiful, but realising that the labourers are few. The mission of the seventy is a kind of parable of the mission of the whole Church. We are commissioned to go out in his name, to travel light, and to speak words of peace in the first instance, and only judge later. As many of us know, it is much easier to judge first, and speak words of peace afterwards! Mission accomplished, the seventy return and report the wonderful deeds that have been done in Jesus' name. Jesus responds with enthusiasm, but gently cautions them against triumphalism. And he prays in the power of the Holy Spirit, with thanksgiving, that the wise and understanding have not had the truth revealed to them, but these babes have, and this was the Father's will.

The second episode is the parable often referred to as the Good Samaritan (Luke 10:25–37). This parable is provoked by a lawyer who asks Jesus what he must do to inherit eternal life. After being asked what is in the Law, the lawyer replies with the *Shema* (the Summary of the Law), words that were known to every devout Jew's heart: 'You shall love the Lord your God with all your heart, and with all your soul, and with all your strength, and with all your mind; and your neighbour as yourself' (cf. Deut. 6:5). This ought to be enough – but it isn't! Again and again, we know what the theory is but we are too blind to put it into practice. So Jesus tells of a man who travels from the holy city down to Jericho, and who – after being beaten up and robbed – is helped by the outcast Samaritan rather than the priest and the Levite, who are intent on keeping their ritual purity, perhaps on their way to Jerusalem for temple worship. The outcast is the one who does the work of God, not the official religious figures.

The third episode has Jesus at the home of Martha and Mary (Luke 10:30–42), two very different sisters. Martha scurries around the house making things ready, like the proverbially pious Jewish woman that she is. But Mary sits at the feet of Jesus, attending to his words. These two contrasting responses could carry on indefinitely, but Martha breaks into the scene by rebuking Mary's apparent refusal to help her in her work. Jesus then reproves Martha, suggesting that she too should listen, and divert her energies and concentration from domestic chores to what he has to teach her, which is far more important.

The life of faith, as told in this part of Luke's Gospel, is therefore about the mission of the seventy, under the grace and authority of Jesus; it is about the Good Samaritan's readiness to give practical help when religious people are busy; and it is about giving proper attention to Jesus' teaching whenever we have the opportunity.

Jesus then goes and prays on his own (Luke 11:1). This is something he does uniquely in Luke's Gospel and on certain specific occasions: at his Baptism (Luke 3:21), after healing (5:16), before calling the disciples (6:12), before Peter's confession of him as the Christ (9:18), before the Transfiguration on the mount (9:28), and in the Garden of Gethsemane (22:41). He prays aloud on other occasions, including when the seventy return (10:21), as well as on the cross itself, when he prays for the forgiveness of those who are crucifying him (23:34) and when he commends himself to the Father at his death (23:46).

This is quite a list. By this stage, Jesus has been observed praying silently five times, and he is about to do so once more in the Garden of Gethsemane. As the disciples at this point see him praying, they ask Jesus to tell them how to pray. In Mathew's Gospel the Lord's Prayer is given as part of his teaching – 'Pray then in this way' (Matt. 6:9a). But here, he is *asked*. The request is significant. The seventy have apparently been successful in their mission, but they have still more to learn, in the parable of the Good Samaritan, in the example of Mary listening at Jesus' feet and in the need to know themselves how they should pray. And no sooner has the prayer ended – in Luke's version with the words 'lead us not into temptation' – than Jesus suggests two particular temptations. The first is to neglect other people's request – prayer – for help: when asked to lend three loaves, we must do so (Luke 11:5ff). And the other temptation is to be timid in our own prayers; we must ask, seek and knock (11:9ff). In other words, when people pray to us for three loaves, even at the most inconvenient time and in the most inconvenient of circumstances, we must give them the basic fare that they ask for if we have it ourselves. Secondly, prayer is about life and must be bold; and more than that, it is about our whole bodies. We ask with our mouths and seek with our eyes and knock with our hands. There could be no clearer hint than this that for Jesus, prayer is no mere verbalizing of received formulas. It is about our whole selves, our whole bodies, our whole lives. For if we ask and seek and knock, we will indeed be given the Holy Spirit (11:13).

\*    \*    \*

We are fortunate in being able to examine both these different sets of terrain. The Lord's Prayer becomes earthed in the narrative of a particular Gospel, and is not seen in isolation from it. The Lord's Prayer is about the secrets of our hearts, as Matthew is at pains to tell us. It is about a life of faith that penetrates those secrets and is not content to make do with outward display. But, as in Luke, the Lord's Prayer is about rooting our lives in being sent out as agents of the gospel, like the seventy. It is about responding to the gospel need even when there are other priorities in the diary. It is about balancing that life in contemplation and action, which belong together and are not about life in separate compartments. Every religious group had its own prayers, and, as the disciples observe Jesus, of course they want to know how they themselves should pray and so the words come forth in their simple profundity.

Some prayers echo these truths, about the opening of the heart, about the penetration of its secrets, and about the need for cleansing by the Holy Spirit, the Father's gift to those who ask. One such prayer was written at the end of the ninth century by Alcuin of York (c.742–804),[4] and was translated into English at the Reformation for use at the Eucharist. Since then it has found its way into Anglican piety and beyond:

Almighty God, to whom all hearts are open, all desires known, and from whom no secrets are hidden; cleanse the thoughts of our hearts by the inspiration of your Holy Spirit, that we may perfectly love you, and worthily magnify your Holy Name; through Jesus Christ our Lord. Amen.

# 3

# Learning the Lord's Prayer

Last night, going to bed alone, I suddenly found myself (I was taking off my waist-coat) reciting the Lord's Prayer, in a loud, emphatic voice – a thing I had not done for many years – with deep urgency and profound and disturbed emotion. While I went on I grew more composed; as if it had been empty and craving and were being replenished, my soul grew still; every word had a strange fullness of meaning which astonished and delighted me. It was late; I had sat up reading; I was sleepy; but as I stood in the middle of the floor half undressed saying the prayer over and over, meaning after meaning sprang from it; overcoming me again with joyful surprise; and I realised that simple petition was always universal and always inexhaustible, and day by day sanctified human life.[1]

Those words were written by the poet Edwin Muir in his personal diary on the first day of March 1939. He had reached a point of crisis in his life – his wife had been seriously ill, and the storm clouds of European war were looming. Under pressure (and what is wrong with pressure?) he found himself returning to a form of words that he had learnt as a boy; and in his autobiography, he noted that on his way home in dejection that evening, he came across some school children playing marbles, just as he had as a boy.

Edwin Muir had a point of reference in his life on which he could draw in that moment of fear, doubt and anxiety. The prayer was already in his bones and suddenly it came to life and the repetitions of the past took on a new meaning. Many of us can identify with that pattern, a pattern of growing up with the prayer, but using it both in private and in public – perhaps realising that more people use it on their own than when gathered for worship! The Edwin Muir model is what many churches have traded on for centuries. The prayer is almost a given part of civilization, and it is there for us to use or come back to, as circumstances allow.

But that world has changed dramatically. One significant indicator is the fact that I seldom preside at a Confirmation service without also having to baptize at least one of the candidates. And whereas when I was a parish priest I often had to reassure these baptism candidates that this was all right, they now come forward as if it is the normal practice, whether they are in their teens, young adults or older people. Moreover the structures of Christian Initiation have had to adapt to a much less uniform scene. When I was a boy, people were baptized as infants, catechized before Confirmation, received their first Communion on some occasions soon after the Confirmation, and somehow were expected to carry on the Christian life! The Book of Common Prayer of 1662 introduced a service of Baptism for those of 'riper years' (unknown in the first Prayer Books in 1549 and 1552) and there has indeed been a steady trickle of such candidates in the centuries since, but nothing like the rise in the last thirty years. So this represents a second kind of new Christian, someone who comes forward who was *not* baptized as an infant. Baptism and Confirmation take place together, usually as part of the Eucharist. This 'all-in-one' model is to be found in antiquity, and it has been recovered in order to deal with our own much changed situation.

But there is a third pattern, which is just as significant. People are baptized and confirmed, and then drift away, and come back, and when they come back, they often want some kind of rite of affirmation; or they come from another Church altogether and want some kind of rite of reception; or there has been some crisis in their lives and they want a rite of reconciliation.[2] The new services of Christian Initiation in *Common Worship* (2000) try to meet the needs that lie behind these diverse patterns, and they look like being a fact of the life and mission of the Church for a significantly long time to come.

Many are the ways in which we can respond creatively to this situation. We need to be much more aware of the very different kind of Church that is being born under our noses than we sometimes are, and nowhere is this truer than in our approach to the Lord's Prayer. I can't remember when I first learnt it, because I grew up with it. But some of the candidates for Confirmation that I meet are often new to the whole repertoire of words and gestures that make up inherited Christian practice and they often show a readiness and enthusiasm that challenge my long-worn habits. In these varied new rites, where there may or may not be a Baptism, and alongside the confirmation there may well be a rite of reception or affirmation, and even possibly one of reconciliation, and there may or may not be a Eucharist, the Lord's Prayer stands out as a unique point of focus, either just before Communion, or – if the service is non-eucharistic – at the end of the intercessions. It always seems like 'returning to base'. The movement and the drama of people coming forward has passed, and we are left with the prayer that Jesus has taught us.

\*   \*   \*

In the early centuries, there grew up a tradition of writing short instructions on the Lord's Prayer for baptism candidates. Some of them are quite short, consisting of a paragraph for each of the petitions, like those delivered by Cyril of Jerusalem (c.315–86), one of the most significant figures of the Eastern Church in the latter part of the fourth century. Cyril was responsible for presiding over the public liturgies in Jerusalem at a time when an increasing number of pilgrims attended. The Lord's Prayer seems to have been a recent introduction to the Eucharist at the time, and people did not recite it publicly at the Eucharist until they had been baptized: non-communicants departed at the end of the liturgy of the Word, and were not allowed to stay. The candidates were instructed in how to recite it before their Baptism, but Cyril's brief instructions as to its meaning were given *after* their Easter Baptism. This provides a significant pattern in itself, which one could almost describe as an acute example of educational psychology. Learn the words before the big event, then recite them for the first time, and only then have the basic meaning explained. There is evidence for other Christian teachers using a similar technique, and in the first part of the sixth century Caesarius of Arles (c.469–542) used a short and pithy explanation of the Lord's Prayer, with a paragraph on each of the petitions.[3]

Another way to heighten the drama, taken up in the new Roman rites of Christian Initiation,[4] is for candidates to recite the Lord's Prayer publicly on the Sunday before their Baptism, usually when they have done the same with the Creed. (This is a revival of an old practice, full of rich provisions for those being baptized at the Easter Vigil, for whom preparation reached a peak of concentration during the preceding Lent.) At this Eucharist, immediately before the Gospel the deacon says, 'Those who wish to learn the Lord's Prayer please come forward.' The celebrant intervenes and speaks to the candidates in words such as 'This is how our Lord taught his disciples to pray.' The deacon then reads the Gospel (Matt. 6:9–13), and in the homily the celebrant is supposed to explain the meaning and importance of the Lord's Prayer. Interestingly, this appears to be the only time that the Lord's Prayer is used as part of the Gospel-reading, thus enhancing its uniqueness.

The ideal picture of the Easter Baptism of candidates, many of them adults, which some early evidence gives us can be misleading. The ancient system, if there ever was a single system, was already breaking down. When, for example, we come across the writings of Justinianus of Valencia in the sixth century, it is assumed that the Lord's Prayer, whilst central to Baptism, will only be learnt afterwards.[5] Sponsors are already being encouraged to teach growing children both the Apostles' Creed and the Lord's Prayer as part of their responsibilities. This is one of the reasons why both figure so prominently in the Prayer Book Catechism, and why in some churches, for example, they were painted, often in elaborate letters along with the Ten Commandments, on the wall on either side of the altar, as a kind of Reformation iconography. Expositions of the Lord's Prayer of different kinds have abounded through the centuries, whether one is thinking of Cyril to the newly baptized after Easter in Jerusalem at the end of the fourth century; or Justinianus of Valencia encouraging the instruction of the growing Christian young, through clergy and god-parents; or the countless ways in which people have seen this prayer's significance by learning from the example of others.

There was, however, a difference between medieval and Reformation piety in this regard. Although in the Middle Ages there were some vernacular versions of the Lord's Prayer, it was always recited 'officially' in the Church's language. In the West this meant Latin, in the East it usually meant Greek, or one of the other recognized tongues such as Syriac. The distance between the Church's Latin and the understanding of ordinary people was acutely felt. There is a story about someone asking Jordan of Saxony (+1237), Master of the Dominican Order, what was the difference between the Lord's Prayer recited by a theologian and a peasant. Jordan replied that the Lord's Prayer was like a precious jewel, which shone out with its own glisten-ing lights, regardless of whether it was in the hands of someone who knew about precious stones or not.[6]

*   *   *

We need to keep hold of this truth, even in an age where the 'distance' between the Church and the culture in which we live is of a different kind from Latin and vernacular. Some would say that the distance is just as great, even though we purport to be speaking the same language! It is also a world in which the whole notion of 'orality' has been changed by the technology of printing and mass-communication, overwhelming the collec-tive memory, and challenging religious practice into a position where common *rhythms* (if not words) become all the more important.[7] That leads me back to the different ways in which people come forward for Baptism and Confirmation, whether they grow up with Christianity, whether they come deliberately

into it, or whether they return to it, rejoin, re-appropriate. The
Lord's Prayer must be part of that process. It must not become
consumerized (as if it ever could!), so that we seem to 'learn' it
like ticking the box, then going on to something else. The
Lord's Prayer is a living expression of the Christian faith as
something which is both supremely obvious and supremely
difficult, easy to repeat in theory, but harder to put into practice
– and certainly to be returned to again and again, as Edwin
Muir himself learnt. When we recite those words, we are doing
so in company with other people for whom the words may well
be startlingly fresh. We have the opportunity to share in that
newness, for – to use Jordan of Saxony's image – we ourselves
might become the ignorant rather than the informed user, even
though its glistening value is a Christian 'given'.

The truth of the matter is that we are never going to learn the
Lord's Prayer fully, yet its most inviting linguistic features are
its rhythmic style, strong in the original Aramaic, strong in the
New Testament Greek, and still strong in the translations into
countless tongues that have emerged ever since. There is one
particular example of a man for whom the Lord's Prayer
seemed to know no bounds in the learning, and for whom it
held a pivotal place in the liturgy. Martin Luther (1483–1546),
the great German reformer, inherited from his Augustinian
formation a deep love of the Lord's Prayer, insisting on the
promises of Christ as the background to faith itself. He wrote
about it frequently, expounding it to different groups, making
it central to his liturgy, and even writing a nine-verse metrical
version of the prayer, 'Vater unser im Himmelreich' (1539), a
melody that has inspired countless organists in the Lutheran
tradition, J. S Bach included, to improvise and reflect. In his
exposition of the Sermon on the Mount, he begins his treatment
of the prayer thus: 'Learn, therefore, that there can be no real
prayer without this faith. But do you feel weak and fearful?
Your flesh and blood are always putting obstacles in the way of
faith, as if you are not worthy enough or ready enough or
earnest enough to pray. Or do you doubt that God has heard
you, since you are a sinner?'[8]

# 4

# Private and Public

At 11.15 pm on New Year's Eve, 1999, the millennium cele-
brations in the Dome at Greenwich placed the spotlight on the
Archbishop of Canterbury leading the Lord's Prayer. There had
been some discussion as to whether it should be allowed into an
occasion which was intended to draw in men and women of all
faiths and none. But in the event, Dr George Carey *did* come
forward, and the prayer was offered in what was probably for
Britain one of its most public forms ever – that is, when one
includes all those who were watching it on television or listening to it on the radio.

But how far is this prayer private and how far is it public? In
both the New Testament accounts, the disciples are given the
prayer *collectively*. In Matthew's version, it comes in the context of teaching about Christian lifestyle, halfway through the
Sermon on the Mount, whereas in Luke's version, the disciples
themselves ask, 'Teach *us* to pray.' There is no doubt that the
Lord's Prayer has carried a greater load of human context and
aspiration over the centuries than any other prayer – and it will
continue to do so. I have prayed that prayer every day, on my
own in my bedroom or in my study or in my chapel. Sometimes
I find it hard to draw a neat distinction between whether it is
'private' or 'public'. The early Christian manual, the *Didache*,
recommends that the Lord's Prayer should be recited three
times each day (*Didache* 8.3). But we cannot be certain whether
this implies a set form of daily prayer or not.[1]

Nor is it clear how and when it came to be recited at the
Eucharist.[2] Evidence suggests that it appeared some time from
the fourth century onwards, which was a time of considerable

standardization as the Church moved more into the public arena from the era of persecution. In the East, the prayer seems to have been recited by all, whereas at Rome, at least for a time, it was recited by the priest on his own. Perhaps the most unusual way of reciting it was in the old 'Visigothic' rite, which was used in Spain until the time of the reconquest after the Muslim occupation, at the end of the Middle Ages. Here, the priest recites each petition on his own, and the congregation respond with an 'Amen'. (The Visigothic rite uses this mannerism of the intercalated 'Amen' for certain other prayers as well, including blessings – a practice that has been revived in recent years.) It is intended to be a way of fixing on the uniqueness and significance of each petition. Several commentators down the ages have drawn attention to the fact that the 'Amen' at the end of the Lord's Prayer applies to each single one of the petitions, and is not intended simply to be a kind of liturgical full stop.

In the Eucharist, the Lord's Prayer in both the ancient Eastern and Western Churches comes between the Eucharistic Prayer and the distribution of Communion and it is easy to see why. It serves as a bridge between the consecration and the reception of the elements. Indeed, one could hardly find a more dramatic position. At the Reformation, Martin Luther simplified the eucharistic liturgy considerably, but retained the Lord's Prayer in this pre-communion position, thus giving it a rare prominence. Thomas Cranmer, on the other hand, took the view that the Lord's Prayer should be recited after the sacramental act, which is why it appears in the Prayer Book immediately after Communion, immediately after Baptism, and also immediately after Confirmation.

As far as the daily offices are concerned, the Lord's Prayer generally comes after the Psalmody and the Readings, as part of a unit of liturgical prayer at the end. But practices vary, almost as if there is a concern to draw attention to its special place. In *The Rule of St Benedict*, at Lauds and Vespers (the two principal offices of the day) the Abbot recites the entire Lord's Prayer on his own, 'for all to hear'. But at other services, it is recited silently, with the whole community only coming in with 'but deliver us from evil'. For the officiant only to recite the prayer, with the petition for deliverance from evil as a response, was standard in the Middle Ages; and the custom from the time, contained in the Prayer Book, was to use the prayer as an introduction to services. Whenever I am given the order of service for a special occasion, I always look carefully at where the Lord's Prayer is placed.

What, then, of these different positions? In the Eucharist, the Lord's Prayer states in a powerful way that every single petition is about the sacrament, as a prayer to the Father, whose name is holy in the holy gifts and the holy people, whose kingdom is celebrated at this table, whose will is fulfilled in the command to 'do this in remembrance of me', who indeed gives us each day the eucharistic bread, through faithful reception and equipping us to forgive others, as well as providing us with sustenance against temptation of whatever kind and against evil. That collective sense of waiting on the Eucharist is heightened when the whole congregation – and not just the clergy – stretch their hands up in the ancient Christian gesture of pleading and prayer. Mention was made earlier of Cranmer's use of the prayer immediately after Baptism. Whether or not he was aware of it, great minds do indeed think alike! In the Syrian and Armenian rites, the Lord's Prayer is recited immediately after Baptism, as a response by the newly baptized themselves for the gift of this new life. Nothing could be more dramatic, particularly when we are considering the close relationship between Baptism, the sacrament of new birth under the fatherhood of God and the recitation of his uniquely 'baptismal' prayer.

\*     \*     \*

Another way to sharpen the focus of the prayer is through the words of introduction. At first sight, it seems a strange thing to do, even in a self-consciously didactic age like ours. But the words of introduction serve the purpose of ensuring that *everyone* comes in with those opening words 'Our Father'. Those

opening words are essential, because the prayer is about the
fatherhood of God, which we share in Christ himself, through
our rebirth in the Holy Spirit. If those words are recited by
someone else as a kind of cue for the rest of the prayer, the
meaning of the words that we pray can become distorted. The
early Christians grasped this point, hence the tradition of using
introductory words. The commonest refer to following the
teaching of Jesus, and this is what has been used for centuries,
and they appear in the revised liturgies as well. In the East,
the introductory words have often referred to forgiveness and
sanctification.

The old Spanish Visigothic rite provides another unusual
example here. Rich in prayers for each occasion, including for
the two main parts of the Eucharistic Prayer, this rite has an 'ad
orationem' ('towards the prayer') which varies as well. They
make interesting reading and probably emerged from a tradition of extemporizing. Usually quite short, they pick up a particular theme of the day, but the commonest is our baptismal
rebirth as children of God, whereby we are to call God 'Father'
(cf.Rom 8:15). Here is the introduction to the Lord's Prayer at
the Easter Vigil:

> Celebrating on this night the most excellent feast of your
> resurrection, O Christ, in which the new day itself, rising
> from the new tomb, has changed the old shadow of ancient
> night into heavenly brightness; with deep weeping, we are
> able to implore you that as you have redeemed us with the
> price of your blood, you will accept the teaching which was
> given by you of our prayer, when we proclaim from earth
> what you yourself have taught us.[3]

The style of Visigothic prayers is usually florid, and this is
neither the shortest in their repertoire, nor is it the longest. A
frequent motif of these compositions is to contrast the heavenly
with the earthly – we pray from earth the prayer of the heavenly
redeemer, just as the Lord's Prayer itself contrasts the earthly
and the heavenly in the doing of the will. These remarkable

formulae perhaps suggest a model for composing short, variable introductions to the Lord's Prayer, which could employ particular baptismal themes, and include as well the fact that Christ himself has taught this prayer to us.

\* \* \*

But there are ways of pointing to the prayer's uniqueness in the domain of private piety. One of these is the devotional paraphrase, prayerful expansions of the different petitions, a practice that developed in the Middle Ages. Such a tradition grew considerably after the Reformation, in both Roman Catholic and Anglican writers. A lengthy series of expansions of each petition of the Lord's Prayer has been attributed to Francis de Sales (1567–1622), a prominent spiritual writer of the Counter-Reformation. Here is one of his sentiments on the petition 'your kingdom come':

> Holy Father, we are banished from your Kingdom, and are in the valley of tears.
>
> O Father, make us return there. As pilgrims long for the last day which will complete their journey and where they will find their city and their homes, so we desire that your kingdom come, in order that our pilgrimage may be completed and that we enter into the place that you have prepared in your holy kingdom.[4]

Another example is William Laud (1573–1645), who was Archbishop of Canterbury at the time of King Charles I and was beheaded for his support of the King. He wrote a paraphrase which reflected his simple but strong faith:

| | |
|---|---|
| Our Father – | Though offended, yet a Father |
| Which art in heaven – | More eminently there, but not there only |
| Hallowed – | In me, by me, upon me, |

| | |
|---|---|
| Be thy name – | The name of a Father in us, that we may become sons of thee our Father |
| Thy kingdom come – | To destroy the kingdom of sin, by which death and the devil reign |
| Thy will be done on earth as it is in heaven – | By me that am but earth, as it is by the holy angels |
| Bread – | The spiritual food of our soul, and also that of our body. |
| Our – | Our own, lawfully gotten, |
| Give us this day our daily bread – | As the necessity of each day requires |
| And forgive us our trespasses, as we forgive them that trespass against us – | Forgive us our talents, who forgive others their pence |
| And lead us not into temptation – | Nor suffer us to enter into temptation, when we are led away and ready to yield to it. |
| But deliver us from evil – | From that author of evil that is without us, the devil, and the world; and from the author of evil that is within us, our own selves; from the evil of sin by thy grace, and from the evil of punishment by thy mercy; from all evil by thy peace. |
| For thine is the kingdom – | Absolute in itself |
| The Power – | Independent on any other |

The Glory –                    Shining round about all things,
                               and in all things: and from thee,
                               and by thee, and to thee, in
                               the glory and salvation of thy
                               servants. Amen.[5]

William Laud reveals here his devotional priorities. He senses
the distance between himself as a weak human being, and the
glory and wonder of the heavenly Father; but the distance is
bridged, because He is not only in heaven, He is on earth as
well. This lays a great responsibility on the believer to take
seriously the call to faithful discipleship. It is the prayer for
deliverance from evil that inspires the longest paragraph, and
may reflect the difficult position that he had at a time when
religion and politics were contriving together to bring England
towards Civil War, for his role as Archbishop of Canterbury
was not uncontroversial. All prayers arise from particular
circumstances. We do not have to enter into the world view or
the circumstances of those who write them in order to make
them our own.

The paraphrase tradition continued unabated, and (one
hopes) will continue in our own time, and beyond. In the early
eighteenth century Thomas Wilson (1663–1755), who was
Bishop of Sodor and Man, wrote no fewer than four paraphrases of the Lord's Prayer for his own private devotions, and
each is distinct in its own right. Such a device has the advantage
of nourishing both the private prayer uttered at the time, and
also its public use. One could say, therefore, that the Lord's
Prayer is a unique and essential link between the two. It is all
about 'our' and 'us' all the way through. But it can be – and
should be – used wherever we are, whether we are on our own
or not. For it is the prayer of Christ in us, in communion with
the whole Church.

# 5

# Overall Shape

There are many ways of describing a prayer. You can talk about its length – how long or short? You can talk about its language – could you understand it? You can talk about its familiarity – was it strikingly different? On all these counts, for most people used to praying, the Lord's Prayer is short, understandable and familiar. But its continuous surprise means that it never ceases to inspire and evoke new boundaries of interpretation.

One way to look at the prayer is its shape: it has a starter, two main sections, and an ending. The Lord's Prayer begins with a starter – 'Our Father in heaven' – and has a conclusion – 'For the kingdom, the power and the glory are yours now and for ever. Amen.' The starter tells us whom we are addressing, and the savoury draws the proceedings to a conclusion. Both are necessary and, like the rest of the prayer, concise. Prayers need beginnings and endings, and what we have in the Lord's Prayer is superb in its simple artistry.

But what of the two main parts of the prayer? Each consists of three petitions. The first is about *God*. 'Hallowed be *your* name, *your* kingdom come, *your* will be done on earth as in heaven.' The second is about *us*. It is right that we start with God before thinking of ourselves. But we then inevitably move into the focus of God's purposes for us. 'Give *us* today our daily bread, forgive *us* our sins, as we forgive those who sin against *us*, lead *us* not into temptation, but deliver *us* from evil.' The whole prayer is addressed to God. Having begun by claiming his fatherhood of us, we pray for the hallowing of his name, the coming of his kingdom, and the doing of his will. Then we move to pray for *our* bread, *our* forgiveness and *our* protection. And we end by ascribing the kingdom, the power, and the glory to God alone. There is a symmetry here, a shape to this unique prayer, a method in its content and direction. In mathematical terms, if we divide the prayer into beginning and ending, and into two sets of three petitions, it comes out as a case of 'three times your' and 'three times our'.

There are further subtleties which the simplicity of the language can yield. The first three petitions are in a different mood (syntax) from the second three, for we say 'hallowed *be* your name' in the sense of asserting this *should* be the case, like *letting* the kingdom come, and letting the will be done. This mood is less assertive, more precatory. But the second three are more like commands: 'give', ' forgive', 'lead us not'. Our 'mood' in addressing God is slightly different in the two main parts of the prayer. *Let* your name be hallowed – because we cannot do it on our own, and it will carry on being hallowed inadequately by others. But *give* us today – because our needs are immediate and specific, and at times desperate. The mood-change is a subtle one, and it only serves to heighten the importance of the two parts of the prayer. For we do not begin with petitions about ourselves and our own particular world, but with the fatherhood, holiness, kingship and will of God himself.

Then there are other correspondences. 'Your will be done on earth *as* in heaven' corresponds with 'forgive us our sins *as* we forgive those who sin against us'. The link between God's will being done on earth *as* it is in heaven suggests that it would be fulfilled if we could forgive others *as* God has forgiven us. The unity of the earthly and the heavenly is the tension that the Christian life walks. We live in a world where the will of God is not done, and where forgiveness is not shared. And since forgiveness is at the centre of the gospel, to forgive other people is a way of doing that will, of drawing heaven and earth into a more complete unity.

Moreover, the will being done 'in heaven' recalls us to the opening of the prayer, which speaks of the Father 'in heaven'. It will be remembered that Luke does not include mention of the Father being in heaven, nor the prayer for the will being done on earth as in heaven (Luke 11:2–4): there is a symmetry in this omission, just as there is a symmetry in their inclusion in Matthew's version. And when we think of the 'kingdom', the 'power' and the 'glory' we can apply these three attributes to earlier parts of the prayer. We have already prayed for the coming of the *kingdom*. The *power* of God is known in the doing of his will. And the *glory* of God is known in his holy name, echoing Jesus' words in the great prayer in the Fourth Gospel, 'Father . . . glorify your Son . . . keep them [the disciples] in your name' (John 17:1,11).

There are other correspondences in the shape of a prayer, in the Jewish piety which would have been deep in Jesus' own prayer life. The first of these is the *Shema* (the Summary of the Law), which comes in different versions in the Gospels, but which – in its original version (Deut. 6:4–5) – tells us that the Lord our God is One and we are to love him with all our heart, soul and strength. The Swedish New Testament scholar, Birger Gerhardsson, has suggested that the *Shema* lies behind much more of the New Testament than has been supposed.[1] As a prayer that Jesus will have recited daily, its threefold sequence of heart, soul and strength could have inspired the 'twice three-fold' character of his own prayer given to the disciples. Can we discern the correspondence? The heart may be there in the hallowing of the name and the daily bread; the soul may be there in the coming of the kingdom and in the gift of forgive-ness; and the strength may be there in the doing of the will and the prayer for protection and deliverance. Other correspond-ences could be found, but that threefold character, with its long tradition of meditation and reflection on the human condition before God, and the way that reflection and meditation leads into faithful servanthood, could have been an inspiration behind the unique structure of this prayer.

Another area of Jewish piety is in the Ten Commandments (Exod. 20:1–17), which would also have been deep in Jesus' own religious life, and which lie behind the teaching that Jesus gives immediately after the Beatitudes in the Sermon on the Mount (Matt. 5:17ff). In the Ten Commandments, it is clear that the first four apply directly to *God*: you shall have no other Gods but me, you shall not make for yourself an idol, you shall not make wrongful use of the name of your Lord your God, remember the sabbath day and keep it holy. All these are about responsible and truthful worship. The remaining six, however, are about responsible and truthful behaviour in the light of the reality of God and his demands on *us*: honour your parents, do not murder, do not commit adultery, do not steal, do not bear false witness, do not covet. The Lord's Prayer likewise begins with a focus on the reality and character of God, and then moves on to how these should be seen in the light of our faithful servanthood. Not every one of those specific commandments can be discerned between the lines of the Lord's Prayer, but such a twofold direction that recognizes God's character and then prays about our own needs has a similar basic movement.

\*  \*  \*

There is, however, yet one more point of comparison. The 'collect' has been a feature on the landscape of Western liturgical tradition since the early centuries. The title could refer to the 'collecting' and focusing of petitions and ideas for the day in one single prayer. The genre has certainly worn well, surviving through the Middle Ages into the Reformation, into both Anglican and Lutheran traditions, and reappearing in a new simpler guise in recent years. One example is the Collect currently used on the second Sunday of Easter in *Common Worship*:

Almighty Father,
you have given your only Son to die for our sins
and to rise again for our justification:
grant us so to put away the leaven of malice and wickedness
that we may always serve you

in pureness of living and truth;
through the merits of your Son Jesus Christ, Our Lord,
who is alive and reigns with you,
in the unity of the Holy Spirit
one God, now and forever.[2]

The structure of this prayer is clear, and becomes clearer
through repetition. This is true not only of itself each year, but
in relation to other collects, which come in the same position, at
the beginning of the Eucharist or towards the end of the daily
offices, week in and week out. The Collect opens with an
*address* to God, 'Almighty Father', and follows with a statement of the *context* in which prayer is offered: 'you have given
your only Son . . .'. Having set the scene, the Collect then moves
into its direct petition, 'grant us so to put away the leaven of
malice and wickedness', which leads into the *purpose* of the
prayer, 'that we may always serve you in pureness of living and
truth.' And it ends in the customary way by praying 'through
Jesus Christ our Lord', but prefixing this with his 'merits',
indicating that this is an Easter prayer, when the focus is on the
fruits of the cross and resurrection. The ending moves into a
Trinitarian formula, which sets our own prayers – 'through
Christ', 'to the Father', 'in the power of the Spirit' – in a style
that goes back to those early centuries.

Collects have to vary, for that is their purpose. Collects have
to fit into a common structure, and consist usually of an opening address, the context of prayer, the petition and purpose of
prayer, and the conclusion. Worshippers need to be helped to
tune into this structure, and sometimes when they are, particularly after many years, they are surprised at what good sense it
makes. But when we compare the Collect with the Lord's
Prayer, we see something yet simpler still. The opening address
is more direct – collects don't always begin 'Almighty Father',
but use other styles as well, such as 'merciful Lord'. The Lord's
Prayer then moves into its context: the hallowing of the name,
the coming of the kingdom and the doing of the will. But these
are expressed as actions of God already, in much the same way

as collects will vary their contexts of prayer: an Epiphany collect will speak of 'the leading of a star' or 'the baptism of Jesus'.

The Lord's Prayer need have no such variation. When it moves into its second part, we make the direct petition by ourselves on behalf the whole world's need for daily bread, for forgiveness, and for protection and deliverance. Collects, on the other hand, vary those needs according to the season and occasion: the Collect for St Columba's Day (9 June) refers to 'your pilgrim people' being 'strong in faith', eminently appropriate when commemorating a missionary saint whose characteristic was courageous travel. And the Lord's Prayer ends by ascribing kingdom and power and glory to God, not praying 'through Jesus Christ', precisely because this prayer's uniqueness lies in the fact that it is Christ's own prayer, where our words are given and spoken by him.

\* \* \*

So the Lord's Prayer lives a life of its own and has a uniqueness that sits somewhat uneasily – in the best sense of the word – alongside other prayers, a uniqueness that is made up of its internal rhythms, with their background in Hebrew poetry, and those striking parallelisms. Something of this genius comes across in a 'Discourse on Prayer' written by Jeremy Taylor (1613–67), one of the greatest Anglican writers of the seventeenth century. In 1649, he published the first ever devotional life of Christ, usually known as *The Great Exemplar*. It is made up of a narrative life of Christ, woven together with other material, including some discourses on particular subjects at appropriate points; his treatment of prayer thus comes after the 'Exposition of The Sermon on the Mount'. These discourses were probably originally sermons which he adapted and expanded for the longer book. Taylor had a knack of getting inside the meanings of things in his own particular way. This is how he expounds the shape of the Lord's Prayer:

In the first petition [hallowed be your Name] the soul puts on the affections of a child, and divests itself of its own interest, offering itself up wholly to the designs and glorifications of God. In the second [your Kingdom come] it puts on the relations and duty of a subject to her legitimate Prince, seeking the promotion of his regal interest. In the third [your will be done . . .] she puts on the affection of a spouse, loving the same love and choosing the same objects; delighting in unions and conformities.

When it comes to the second part of the prayer, Taylor writes as follows:

In these last petitions, which concern ourselves, the soul hath affections proper to her own needs; as in the former proportion, to God's glory. In the first of these [give us today] the affection of a poor indigent and necessitous beggar; in the second [forgive . . .] of a delinquent and penitent servant; and in the last [lead us not . . .] the person in affliction or danger.[3]

Behind the language, which can appear to our own age quaint, and the social context (Taylor was a strong monarchist and 1649 was the year of the execution of Charles I), Taylor's exposition emerges with clarity in the roles which he employs. The child divests itself of its own interest; the subject becomes dutiful to its monarch; the spouse wants to take on the same love, in union and conformity to her married partner. Then the beggar asks for bread, the servant asks for forgiveness, and when we are in affliction or danger, we ask for protection and deliverance. As child, subject, spouse, and as beggar, servant and afflicted, we stand before God, seeing the difficulties around us, but still believing.

# 6

# Summary of the Gospel

When was the first sermon ever preached on the Lord's Prayer? It is impossible to tell, but my suspicions are not long after Christians started praying the prayer, therefore within the lifetime of the New Testament. But the trouble is that nothing has come down to us until we come to Tertullian (c.160–c.225), who lived in North Africa, in what is now Algeria, in the latter part of the second century. His is the first known discourse dealing with the Lord's Prayer. Probably written between 200 and 206, this work is short and clear, and it was read by many people after him, because it has a freshness and a simplicity that reaches across the boundaries of language, culture and time. Near the beginning, he refers to the Lord's Prayer as a 'summary of the gospel',[1] and this description has been used repeatedly ever since. It may not have been his own invention, but that does not matter. The description fits, because in the Lord's Prayer we find a rare penetration of all that Jesus taught and stood for and did.

We have already noted the two versions of the prayer as they appear in Matthew (Matt. 6:9–13), and the shorter version in Luke (Luke 11:2–4). We have noted the fact that each reflects its own characteristics. Matthew is more aware than the other gospel writers of the trials that await those who follow Christ (Matt. 13:31–43,47–50), hence his use of the words 'but deliver us from evil', which do not appear in Luke. Matthew is also keen on mutual forgiveness (Matt. 16:27; 18:23–25), hence his slightly stronger accent on this aspect of discipleship than Luke, and he follows the Lord's Prayer immediately with a warning that we should forgive each other (Matt. 6:14–15).

Luke, on the other hand, sets his giving of the prayer in the context of Christ's own prayer, a particular feature of his Gospel. His petition for *daily* bread is sharper than Matthew's and echoes his call on the disciples, two chapters earlier, to take up their cross *daily* and follow him (Luke 9:23).

We have understandably concentrated on these two Gospels. But what of the other two, in which the Lord's Prayer does not appear at all?[2] This may appear an odd question at first sight, but it needs to be noted carefully. There is so much that is basic to the Christian story which appears in some way or another in each one of the Gospels, such as Christ's teaching, his miracles, and above all the great drama of Christ's passion, which occupies more space than anything else in each of the four.

Mark's Gospel may not contain the Lord's Prayer explicitly, but nearly all of it finds an echo somewhere. Taking each petition, it is easy to see why. Jesus addresses God as 'Abba' in the Garden of Gethsemane (Mark 14:36) with a striking intimacy. At the very beginning of the Gospel, Jesus is there to proclaim the coming of the kingdom (1:14–15), as indeed John the Baptist teaches; and his parables indicate exactly that beginning with the parable of the sower (4:1–20). Jesus, back in the Garden of Gethsemane, wrestles with the doing of the will in the context of temptation (14:32–42). This echoes not only 'your will be done on earth as in heaven' but also 'lead us not into temptation but deliver us from evil', in the second part of the prayer.

What of the giving of daily bread? This can be seen in the two miracles of Jesus feeding the multitudes (6:35–49; 8:1–9), for he who feeds the thousands in the wilderness is the provider of daily bread; and food is a recurrent theme in Mark, sustenance on the road of discipleship. Mark teaches perhaps more firmly than any other Gospel writer about the need to forgive each other, just as our heavenly Father will forgive us, and he does so shortly after the cleansing of the temple, in a saying about the importance of praying (11:25–26). If we add up all those references, they bring us to almost every single word of the Lord's Prayer. The only exception is 'hallowed be your name', which is such a deeply Jewish theme of prayer that its absence in Mark need not strike us as an omission. After all, Jesus' name of Saviour is the expression of the mission and message of God among his people, but – particularly in Mark's Gospel – it is a secret that even the disciples themselves find impenetrable, right to the end.

We thus have an interesting picture. Mark's Gospel, the briefest of the four, does not give us an explicit version of the Lord's Prayer at all. But the teaching of the Lord's Prayer lies between its lines, in some places obviously, in other places less so. Some will interpret this as a sign of Mark's brevity, and the fact that other Gospels elaborate, whether using Mark as a source or other collections of sayings from elsewhere. Another explanation is that the community which used Mark's Gospel either knew the Lord's Prayer already, or were unfamiliar with it, and it was written at a time when some communities were using the prayer and others were not. The salient point, however, is that Mark's Gospel is implicitly compatible with every single syllable of the Lord's Prayer, and that is of some significance in itself. Moreover, its absence from Mark may reflect, too, the fact that Mark does not have the discourse pattern of teaching that we find in Matthew and Luke, and emphasizes the secret character of Jesus' identity.

\* \* \*

John's Gospel, on the other hand, gives us more than Mark, and nearly all of it is located in the lengthy prayer of Christ on the eve of his passion, which has sometimes been called the 'High Priestly Prayer' (John 17). John's Gospel is the longest of the four, and this is the longest prayer put into the mouth of Jesus in the whole of the New Testament. But there is one exception: the prayer for daily bread is not found here, but lies lightly concealed in the feeding of the five thousand in the wilderness. After Jesus has explained that 'the bread of God is that which comes down from heaven and gives life to the world', the disciples reply, 'Sir, give us this bread always' (John 6:33–4). The teaching in that miracle in John's Gospel walks the same fine dividing line between the physical and the spiritual as subsequent interpretations of the prayer for daily bread across the centuries.

What of the rest of the Lord's Prayer in John? The prayer of Christ begins with the words, 'Father, the hour has come' (John 17:1), and it refers to *heaven* as the place where Jesus was with the Father and to which he is to return (17:11; 21:24–5). Jesus prays that his disciples may be kept in the Father's *name* (17:11); and he prays for the *coming of the kingdom* by asking the Father to glorify the Son, since he is being given power over all flesh (17:1–2). The petition for the *doing of God's will* is echoed when Jesus states that he is glorified by the Father on earth, having accomplished the work given him to do (17:4). An allusion to the *forgiveness of sins* may be found in those unique words of Jesus when he asks that his disciples may be sanctified in the truth (17:17). The context and atmosphere mean that what corresponds to being *protected from temptation and delivered from evil* is spread over a number of verses, especially where he prays for the protection and deliverance of his followers, and for their unity (17:11–15).

A different question, however, needs to be asked in relation to the absence of the Lord's Prayer in John. Mark's brevity is a partial explanation in his case. But John's Gospel is far longer. It contains longer teaching by Jesus than the other three, particularly in the so-called 'farewell discourses' (John 13–17). The character of the fourth Gospel needs to be taken into careful consideration. There is no direct narrative of the Baptism of Christ, only a retrospective account by John the Baptist, different in style from the other three Gospels (1:29–34). There is no institution narrative at the Last Supper but, instead, the washing of the feet (13:1–11). Yet baptismal and eucharistic imagery are to be found in the fourth Gospel, for example in the teaching about living water at the encounter with the Samaritan woman (4:7–15), and in the teaching about the bread of life after the feeding of the five thousand (6:35). The community associated with the fourth Gospel probably did not know the Lord's Prayer, but they would have known its teaching, particularly as expressed in the 'High Priestly Prayer' of Jesus (17). If there is an oddity at all, it lies in the fact that the one petition not explicitly found in this chapter is that of daily bread. Yet Jesus, the living bread (6:35), is the one that speaks to the Father and pleads for the continual presence of all that he meant among his disciples. The fourth Gospel, then, in its characteristically more lengthy style, can be said to embody the Lord's Prayer in this unique chapter. And as the four Gospels themselves began to circulate more widely and to be shared among the early Christians, so the version in Matthew's Gospel won through by some kind of consent, doubtless based on its rhythms and brevity, as witness the lightly adapted version of Matthew's words in the *Didache*.

\* \* \*

But there are wider issues concerning the Lord's Prayer as a 'summary of the gospel', so aptly described by Tertullian. These concern the character of the prayer as an embodiment of the Christian good news as a whole. Each petition expresses that gospel in a particular way. The fatherhood of God is about relationality, our relationship with God and with each other. The hallowing of God's name is about worship and mutual respect. The coming of the kingdom is about the authority of God which is both vulnerable and conquering – a paradox that the Church has to face every Holy Week and Easter, and which the human race can face every day. The doing of the will is about a kind of assertion and purposefulness that relates as much to what we do as the way we do it, and it can be as mysterious as our lives often turn out to be. The gospel is about all these truths – relationality, respect, authority and purpose. It is about living and rediscovering that relationality, most fundamentally when it is broken or under strain. There can be a silence about the cross that the human race finds tantalizing.

Our capacities to worship God and to respect each other are interrelated. It is not for nothing that the old formula in the

Prayer Book at the giving of the ring at marriage contains the words 'with my body I thee worship'. Of course worship can turn into its own form of idolatry, so that God becomes a personal or social construct, even a religious system, and our fellow human beings become either idolized in themselves or disregarded and dehumanized. In a world that rightly suspects authority, particularly in historic institutions, there has to be some kind of self-authentication, an authority that 'earns its keep', before people will readily accept its truth and its reality. The gospel teaches us repeatedly that Jesus enters any world, with all its strengths and weaknesses, and he takes on those suspicions, including the capacity for any age to claim its own distinctiveness in relation to any other! And the doing of that will with purpose, enthusiasm and courage means a walk of rediscovery, rather than the grand scheme – or the public relations 'own goal' in a decision that breaks trust by letting go of long-standing loyalities.

The second part of the prayer is equally shot through with the message of the gospel, starting with the problem of our own daily needs, temporal as well as spiritual: daily bread. The gospel is about living faithfully and not necessarily knowing what every single step is going to be; the disciples appear to have left the tomb 'afraid' (Mark 16:8), which implies a truth about fearful lack of foreknowledge as a foundation for growing faith that is consistently overlooked. The prayer for forgiveness takes us straight to the cross, and to the essential metaphors which the New Testament built up in order to express its meaning, whether in justification, a metaphor from the law courts (Rom. 3:21–5), redemption as a metaphor from the slave market (Rom. 8:23) or reconciliation as a metaphor from the Jewish Day of Atonement (Rom. 5:11). And as with daily bread, that repertoire of metaphors has not been exhausted so far. The prayer for protection and deliverance has always been particularly heartfelt by Christians undergoing persecution or trial of one sort or another. Faith is not an anaesthetic intended to dull pain temporarily. It is rather a way of facing the sometimes hard realities of daily living. Luke's

Gospel, one which often shows the most tender side of human nature, includes no fewer than seven warnings not to be afraid, the first three angelically to Zechariah, Mary and the shepherds (Luke 1:13,30; 2:10), the remaining four from Jesus to his followers (Luke 5:10; 8:50; 12:7,32). The doxology, whilst not part of the original version, is none the less a gospel statement in itself, since our lives of praise follow on from our concern with the present (daily bread), our remorse for the past (forgiveness of sins), and our fear of the future (prayer for protection and deliverance).

The Lord's Prayer as 'a summary of the gospel' invites us to live with all the tensions of the life of faith. Austin Farrer (1904–68), one of the most remarkable Oxford teachers of his age, once expressed this aptly:

> An overmastering sense of human ills can be taken as the world's invitation to deny her Maker, or it may be taken as God's invitation to succour his world. Which is it to be? Those who take the practical alternative become more closely and more widely acquainted with misery than the onlookers; but they feel the grain of existence, and the movement of the purposes of God. They do not argue, they love; and what is love is always known as good. The more we love, the more we feel the evils besetting or corrupting the object of our love. But the more we feel the force of the besetting harms, the more certain we are of the value residing in what they attack; and in resisting them are identified with the action of God, whose mercy is over all flesh.[3]

# 7

# Vain Repetition?

'Vain repetitions' is an expression questioning set forms of prayer that are used without proper understanding. The words come from the Authorised Version of the Bible (1611) when Jesus says, just before giving the disciples the Lord's Prayer, 'But when ye pray, use not vain repetitions, as the heathen do: for they think that they shall be heard for their much speaking' (Matt. 6:7). Interestingly, the versions of the previous century by William Tyndale and Miles Coverdale both use the word 'babble', which suggests empty phrases, and that is how modern translations tend to translate it. What Jesus is criticizing is not only inordinate length but words that are not understood. And this provides a more than adequate platform on which to launch what is probably the briefest and richest prayer ever composed.

But that has not stopped Christians down the ages from approaching it with a certain degree of circumspection, not to say – at times – scepticism. In the Eucharist, the Lord's Prayer is usually carefully introduced, pointing out that these are words that Jesus has taught us. And there are many parts of the Christian world where it is not allowed to end without an interjection from the priest picking up the petition for protection against evil, which begins 'deliver us, Lord, from every evil . . .'. Those who have written or preached about the Lord's Prayer have taken care to expand on its meanings in order to kindle the imaginations of worshippers in such a way that they themselves can bring their all to these words, whether spoken aloud in public, or uttered in the heart in private.

\* \* \*

The most severe approach to the Lord's Prayer, however, came at the Reformation. John Calvin (1509–64), the leader of the Reformed Church in Geneva, deftly uses it as the basis of his teaching about the meaning of all prayer, and the forms of services emanating from Geneva made provision of it, but mainly in a lengthy paraphrase as the intercession after the sermon. In his *Institutes of the Christian Religion*, he criticizes formality and insincerity: 'It is perfectly clear that neither words nor singing (if used in prayer) are of the least consequence, or avail one iota with God, unless they proceed from deep feeling in the heart.' And he goes on to describe the Lord's Prayer as 'a form which is set before us as in a picture, everything which it is lawful to wish, everything which is conducive to our interest, everything which is necessary to demand'.[1]

There were clearly many who were wary about the repetition of set prayers, even this one, and when the (Presbyterian) Westminster Directory was issued in 1645, which replaced the Prayer Book during the commonwealth under Oliver Cromwell, more defensiveness enters the scene. In the directions concerning morning worship, topics for the prayer after the sermon are suggested, after which comes the following suggestion: 'and because the Prayer, which Christ taught his Disciples, is not only a Pattern of Prayer, but itself a most comprehensive Prayer, we recommend it also to be used in the Prayers of the Church.'[2] An eloquent Puritan, Thomas Watson (+1686), wrote what is probably one of the longest expositions of the Lord's Prayer, running to over three hundred pages of close print. It is marked by earnestness and liveliness of style, but on the first page he notes that Jesus does not say, 'after these *words*, pray ye,' but 'after this *manner*' (Matt. 6:9a). With characteristic directness, he states that 'the Ten Commandments are the Rule of our Life, the Creed is the sum of our faith, and the Lord's Prayer is the pattern of our prayer'. There is clearly some sensitivity in the atmosphere both in what Calvin wrote, in what the Directory says, and in what Thomas Watson has written. Why?

The reasons are not hard to find. In medieval Catholic devotion, the rosary had long been used for counting the number of times the Lord's Prayer was recited, and in many religious communities, lay brothers who could not read repeated the Lord's Prayer through the rosary and regarded that as equivalent to the recitation of the Psalter. (Fifteen decades of the rosary multiplied by ten reaches the number one hundred and fifty.) It was only in the twelfth century that the practice began of adding or substituting the 'Hail Mary' (Luke 1:28), with or without the conclusion asking for her prayers.

There was a tradition, too, of interpreting the Lord's Prayer in an allegorical manner. One example is a work by Hugh of Amiens (c.1085–1164), entitled *Concerning the Catholic Faith and the Lord's Prayer*, which was probably written between 1155 and 1159, when Hugh was Archbishop of Rouen.[3] He produces an elaborate scheme which identifies each one of the seven orders of the church (presbyter, deacon, subdeacon, acolyte, exorcist, reader and doorkeeper) with one of the seven petitions of the Lord's Prayer, one of the seven gifts of the Holy Spirit, and one of the Beatitudes! (Like many commentators, he distinguished 'lead us not into temptation' from 'deliver us from evil', which Calvin insisted on drawing together.) For example, Hugh drew together for presbyters the spirit of wisdom (Isa. 11:2), the first petition of the Lord's Prayer ('hallowed be your name'), and the seventh beatitude about peacemakers (Matt. 5:9).[4] Calvin and the other Reformers were not enamoured by what they saw as a mechanical use of Christ's words, nor by what they believed was a false interpretation, particularly (as in the case of Hugh) when it seemed to be worked out to bolster up a series of orders in the Church that had for them no scriptural foundation.

A similar defensiveness is clear from the opening words of a series of sermons preached in 1552 on the Lord's Prayer by one of the leading lights of the English Reformation, Hugh Latimer (1490–1555). Latimer begins as follows: 'I have entered of late in the way of preaching, and spoken many things of prayer, and rather a prayer than of any other thing: for I think there is nothing more necessary to be spoken of, nor abused than prayer was by the craft and subtlety of the devil; for many things were taken for a prayer when they were nothing less. Therefore at this time also I have thought it good to entreat of prayer, to the intent that it might be known how precious a thing right prayer is.'[5] Many others preached courses of sermons on the Lord's Prayer at the Reformation, and many of them, like Latimer, had a fluency which owed a great deal to the enthusiasm of it now being officially accessible in the native tongue.

The situation in England became more complex still, for two reasons. The first was that the Prayer Book directed the Lord's Prayer to be recited twice at Morning and Evening Prayer, and at the Holy Communion. The first time at Morning and Evening Prayer, the priest was to recite it, the people following him after each petition. Then later on at Morning and Evening Prayer, everyone was supposed to say it together. At the Eucharist, however, the priest was to say it on his own at the start, but after Communion, they were to repeat every petition after him, as at the start of Morning Prayer. Since that time, there has been a tendency in Prayer Book services to omit the first recitation and concentrate on the second, always said by all together. But these deliberately different directions were intended to embed the prayer in the consciousness of the people with different usages of the same words. Towards the end of the sixteenth century, Thomas Cartwright (1535–1603) attacked reciting the Lord's Prayer twice, particularly doing so phrase after phrase with the minister. Richard Hooker (1554–1600), on the other hand, who was one of the leaders of the late Elizabethan Church, defended the practice, since he regarded the Lord's Prayer as central, enabling worshippers to think more about its importance and meaning. Cartwright, like many of the Puritans of his time, preferred long extempore prayers, and found the Prayer Book constricting. Hooker, in turn, found such a style tedious and he believed that it was at them, rather than at him, that Jesus' warning about 'babbling' was really directed! He had, moreover, a veneration for a prayer that Jesus himself uttered and taught his disciples which is beautifully expressed in the following words (echoing 1 Cor. 13:1): 'Though men should speak with the tongues of angels, yet words so pleasing to the ears of God as those which the Son of God himself hath composed were not possible for men to frame.'[6]

The controversy, of course, was a complex one. There were no doubt adherents of the Prayer Book who found strange the different ways of reciting the Lord's Prayer and doing so twice. There were also Puritans who, while keen on the private use of the prayer, also found its recitation in public services more than odd. But there was a more radical alternative discernible already between the lines of Calvin and the Westminster Directory, which was sceptical about its use at all, whether in private or public. For them, the Lord's Prayer was Christ's own words, and it was presumptuous of us to take them for granted, still less to make them our own. We should indeed base our own prayers on its pattern and structure, but such prayers that we use should vary from occasion to occasion, rather than be read out of a book. For example, the radical Puritan, Philip Nye (c.1596–1672), strongly recommended its total disuse. Every shift in the life of the Church produces its own reactions, and it is easy for us, who live at such a distance from these events, to see that the medieval Catholic edifice was ripe for change.

\* \* \*

Since those days, we have learnt to learn from each other. Anglicans have more freedom in their liturgy than they had before, and many of the heirs of the Puritan tradition, including Presbyterians, are more at ease about set forms of service. In our own age, sometimes characterized by the need for self-expression, the Lord's Prayer can take on a life of its own and can warn us against turning prayer into another kind of vain repetition, or even a repeat performance of the sermon. The gospel imperative is that all our praying should stand under the spotlight of what we find in the Gospels given by Jesus himself, and that is what John Calvin was trying to get across.

Nevertheless, whether Jesus is warning us against 'babbling' at inordinate length, or even against repeating set formulae in an empty way, the self-critical tradition of Christian experience should not be ignored simply because some of the lessons of the Reformation – on both sides – have been redressed. Anglicans no longer need to employ the somewhat contrived ways of reciting the Lord's Prayer in the Prayer Book in order to be relaxed in its public recitation. Roman Catholics, on the other hand, now have the freedom to recite the Pater Noster (as the Reformers themselves frequently called it, as a widely accepted nickname) in their own tongue. They have the opportunity to explore the full range of its meaning as it is encountered by them in an English translation rather than the Latin.

There will always be those who are uncomfortable, whether permanently or temporarily, with this prayer. The Quaker tradition, itself a significant and subtle form of liturgical protest, waits in silence upon God and is content to remain still and to trust words only when they are really necessary or when someone is moved to utter them. In that context, the Lord's Prayer remains part of scripture, operating less as a formula to be recited which the Church has found useful, and more as a light shining from a distance on an ongoing discipleship, in which contemplation and action mingle in a sophisticated manner in the stillness of the meeting-room.

There are those, too, who have given up reciting the Lord's Prayer – for a time. They may rely on others to recite it for them and their reluctance to recite it may be related to a wider but temporary reluctance about any form of prayer at all. It is as if the soul is rebelling against the collective inheritance. The rebellion may be provoked by a crisis of faith of a temporary kind, or an inner conviction that these words are too sacred to mean anything specific at the time, or even that the soul must fast from such fare for a time.

But there are also those for whom the Lord's Prayer emerges as its own defence against petitions that are vain and babbling that is unedifying. In any case, when do we really mean what we are saying? Few of us would want to make any special claim for the quality of our prayers, however attached we may be to our favourites. But when we come to the Lord's Prayer, we are – as it were – coming home. For there is a secret and hidden power in repetition, because it brings into the unconscious what the external world feeds it.

When I was staying with a Greek Orthodox religious community, I noticed a rosary, tucked up a sleeve of one of the monks. It looked like a small fancy rope with a tassel at the end. I subsequently bought one and discovered that it was made up of four sets of twenty-five black knots, each joined by a single knot in pale beige. The sets of twenty-five are for the Jesus prayer, 'Lord Jesus, Son of the living God, have mercy on me a sinner.' The larger knots are for the Lord's Prayer. I can still recall the monk standing there, counting the knots. For every twenty-five times that he asked for God's mercy, he prayed the Lord's Prayer once. The whole exercise I found immediately appealing. It shook me out of my Western individualism, with its suspicion of the embodied, physical character of Christian devotion and its (at times) over-concentration on the individual and the verbal. Here was no vain repetition, no heaping up of unnecessary words. Here was the Lord's Prayer, lightly coloured and full of heaven, in the midst of a weak but redeemed humanity, asking for mercy and healing.

# 8

# Following Christ

'As our Saviour Christ hath commandeth and taught us, we are bold to say . . .'

These are the words which introduced the Lord's Prayer whenever I went to Communion as a boy from my earliest years. They are what appear in the Scottish Book of Common Prayer (1929). They are deeply embedded in my memory, and they have travelled with me into many other communities. These communities include those I have visited as a friend, when I have listened to the ancient language of Estonia, or those which I have visited in mind and spirit, as when I have read the Lord's Prayer in such differing North American tongues as Mohawk or one of the Inuit dialects. That set of experiences is a varied tapestry, and it makes one conscious of the different versions that have been used, wherever we are, and the need for trust and agreement – as well as patience – when a new translation has to emerge. But whenever we read, there is a sense in which we are also translating, especially in a prayer that is full of such metaphors as name, kingdom, will, bread, forgiveness, and protection.[1]

It took some time before the full meaning of the words 'we are bold to say' dawned on me. Why on earth should we be 'bold' when reciting the Lord's Prayer? I did understand the importance of an introductory formula. It seemed to mean that we should all come in with those opening words 'Our Father', which makes me object when whoever presides at a service goes straight into the opening words, as if they were a cue, and no more.

But there is a necessary 'boldness' about uttering those words at all. We are bold because we can dare to address God as Father, in the same way that Jesus did himself. That 'boldness' is fundamentally about our character as reborn children of God, a fact made all the more apparent in the bodily posture of standing. Preaching on the Sermon on the Mount, delivered in 1748, John Wesley (1703–91), the great evangelist, had this to say about the Lord's Prayer:

> We may observe in general concerning this divine prayer, first, that it contains all that we can reasonably or innocently pray for. There is nothing which we have need to ask of God, nothing which we could ask without offending him, which is not included either directly or indirectly in this comprehensive form. Secondly, that it contains all we can reasonably or innocently desire; whatever is for the glory of God, whatever is needful or profitable, not only for ourselves, but for every creature in heaven and earth. And indeed our prayers are the proper test of our desires. Nothing being fit to have a place in our desires which is not fit to have a place in our prayers; what we may not pray for, neither shall we desire. Thirdly, that it contains all our duty to God and man; whatsoever things are pure and holy, whatsoever God requires of the children of men, whatsoever is acceptable in his sight, whatsoever is whereby we may profit our neighbour, being expressed or implied therein.[2]

\*    \*    \*

Time and again I am brought back to the figure of Jesus of Nazareth, and the differing accounts given of his life and ministry in the four Gospels. We have seen some of the possible influences that Jesus as a devout Jew will have known, such as the *Shema* (the Summary of the Law) and the *Decalogue* (the Ten Commandments). But there were other influences, from Jewish prayers which Jesus will have known from attending synagogue. One is the so-called *Kaddish*. Known in various longer versions including for commemorating the departed, it was used by the synagogue preacher at the end of his discourse, and was – and is – like the *Shema*, part of the life of every devout Jew. We do not know exactly the version familiar to Jesus, but it may have taken the following form:

> Magnified and sanctified be his great name in the world which he hath created according to his will. May he establish his kingdom during your life and during your days, and during the life of all the house of Israel, even speedily and at a near time, and say ye, Amen. Let his great name be blessed for ever and to all eternity.[3]

The *Kaddish* is thought to be very ancient, and, although prayed in Hebrew, has some signs of Aramaic origins. Along with its brevity, and the fact that it prays about the name and the kingdom, it is thus the closest parallel that we have betweeen the Lord's Prayer and Jewish prayer.

Another set of prayers are the 'Eighteen Benedictions', which are appointed to be recited daily at the synagogue, 'Blessed art thou, O Lord our God . . .' Unlike the *Kaddish*, the 'Eighteen' are responsive, and are much longer. They share certain common themes, such as the reference to God as our father, the holiness of the name, and the prayer for forgiveness. Like the Lord's Prayer in the *Didache*, the 'Eighteen Benedictions' are recommended to be recited three times a day.

The Lord's Prayer thus emerges from its roots in Jewish piety, the praying milieu which Jesus himself knew. But it is untypical, because – with the exception of the *Kaddish* – it is so short. And it also lacks three other ingredients common in Jewish prayer: thanksgiving, lament and blessing.[4] Perhaps this is another indication of its uniqueness. John Wesley is not the only writer to draw attention to its brevity, but he sees with his customary penetrating eye that our prayer should be tested by the Lord's Prayer, and so should our human desires as well.

The prayer only appears in two of the Gospels, and in two different versions, but there are enough echoes in the Gospels of

Mark and John for us to be satisfied that this really is in every sense a prayer of the Gospels, a following of Christ. We have to keep searching for origins of the prayer, and we have to be ready to face new truths and let our perspectives shift and change, and that includes our greater knowledge of the background of the prayer than previous centuries, as well as our growing knowledge of its different liturgical uses, and the motivations that gave rise to those uses. Indeed, part of that following of Christ is about making sense of such a quest – in the New Testament, and in the wider liturgical tradition. Some bygone ages would never have thought it necessary to search John 17 and find much of it between the lines of Jesus' words of prayer to the Father on the night of his arrest. But the following of Christ must take us back to measuring our own prayers by the Lord's Prayer itself. Charles Gore (1853–1932), a great Anglican theologian and writer, expounded the Sermon on the Mount in Lent and Easter 1895 in Westminster Abbey, and was led to remark as follows:

> Therefore, as this Lord's Prayer represents profoundly and perfectly the spirit of Him who first spoke it, and who taught it to His Church, it follows that it is beyond all other prayers, the prayer in Christ's name. Who then wants to know whether this or that thing can be prayed for in Christ's name? The answer is to be found in another question, can it be legitimately covered by the clauses of the Lord's Prayer?[5]

The Lord's Prayer stands beside those utterances recorded in the Gospels where Jesus spoke directly to his Father in heaven. Some of the blending that was taking place in the formation of the two versions may have resulted from the early Church settling down to living in history, rather than expecting the sudden return of Christ. Our primary concern as users of this prayer is not to be surprised by the perhaps random way in which a single version might have appeared. In any case, there will be new translations, just as there were in the past. Our very use of this prayer in so many different contexts requires these attitudes. For it is *our* prayer, not just the Lord's Prayer, or the prayer of a nostalgic church that we once knew, or the work of a translator who lived long ago whom we happen to like.

'As our Saviour taught us, so we pray . . .' This is the commonest cue today, in the simplicity of modern English. The Lord's Prayer is both beautiful words and a prayer of faith. William Tyndale (c.1484–1536), who gave his life in 1536 for daring to translate the scriptures into clear and resonant English, captured this truth when he wrote: 'Now, God looketh not on the pain of the prayer but on thy faith and his promise and goodness'.[6]

*   *   *

The Lord's Prayer is a way of following Christ. It is a prayer that leads us back to each one of the Gospels themselves, given to us explicitly in the Sermon on the Mount in Matthew; implicitly in the starkness of Mark; taught us directly in Luke at the request of the disciples themselves; and spread through the 'High Priestly Prayer' of the fourth Gospel. It is a prayer that is Trinitarian, for it is Christ's prayer to the Father, in words which we can only utter in the power of the Spirit. It is, too, a prayer of costly discipleship, for each one of its petitions has a cutting edge, in a world where our names and our identities are constantly profaned; where authorities vie for assertiveness; where wilfulness takes over from sacrifice; where daily sustenance is for millions seldom a reality; where the depth of sin is often carefully tallied rather than lovingly remitted; and where dangers of our own making and folly continue to rob the world of its fullest potential. Our dependence on God and one another is what this prayer is about. As William Beveridge (1637–1708), one of the devotional writers of his age, puts it at the start of his own treatment of the Lord's Prayer: 'He that is not sensible of his own weakness, will never look out for help'.[7]

So many of the sentiments of people who have written on the Lord's Prayer down the ages have – at their best – concentrated on its *use*, and this is the note that needs to be struck now,

before we go on to look at each petition in turn. In 1592, the
leading English Puritan, William Perkins (1558–1602) wrote
an exposition of the Lord's Prayer. At the time a popular
preacher in Cambridge whose works were noted for their learning and plainness, Perkins was able to reach a wide religious
market. This particular book went through four editions in five
years, and was translated into Dutch in 1603, German in 1606,
and Welsh in 1677. Towards the end he writes as follows:

> The principal use of the Lord's Prayer is to direct God's
> church in making their prayers in all places, at all times, and
> upon all occasions, though their prayers should be innumer-
> able: and unless they be framed after this, they cannot be
> right.
>
> In the using of it for direction he that would pray it must
> understand the meaning thereof, the wants therein to be
> bewailed, and the grace to be desired, for which end it hath
> been expounded.[8]

Perkins wants to make as much as he can of the words of the
prayer in order that his hearers may live lives of greater holiness
and usefulness under God. Time and again, I have watched
people being surprised by something that they have said and
apparently known for years, and a new shade of meaning, a
new application to themselves, has dawned upon them. We
need to breathe in that kind of patience – patience with
ourselves, patience with the equipment that has been given
us (prayers included), and above all patience with God. As
followers of Christ, we have to start where we are, and realise
that by the invitation of these words, we do indeed have a new
and living way to enter the sanctuary by the blood of Jesus, with
boldness (Heb. 10:19).

# PART TWO

# Meanings

# 9

# Our Father in Heaven

On my father's seventieth birthday, the grandchildren decided
to present him with a small silver goblet and, in order to show
it was from them, they decided to have inscribed around the
bowl the names which they used to call him. In typical family
fashion, the three branches of the family produced three different names: Pop, Pater and Abba. Pop is short for papa, and has
been used in this country for a long time. Pater is the Latin for
father, and is equally traditional, though a little Victorian.
Abba, however, is the Aramaic for father, the word Jesus himself uses on one occasion in the Gospels.

But the meaning of the word is not simply 'father' in a
descriptive fashion. All these terms try to reflect both an intimacy and a respect: an intimacy that is not about patronizing or
trivializing the other person, and a respect that is not about
terror and dread. Every language seems to try to come up with
such a form of intimate but respectful address for one's father
and mother. Some time ago, the German scholar, Joachim
Jeremias suggested that 'Abba' corresponded to something like
the English 'daddy'. This tips the balance more in the direction
of intimacy than respect, and in recent years, James Barr has
argued that 'Abba' in New Testament times corresponds
more to 'papa', with its overtones of nearness combined with
distance.[1]

In the New Testament, this Aramaic word 'Abba' appears
untranslated in the Greek, immediately followed by 'father',
three times. First of all, Jesus uses it in the Garden of
Gethsemane, at the moment of crisis: 'Abba, Father, for you all
things are possible' (Mark 14:36). That is the only time in the

Gospels, and it seems to have been put there deliberately in order to heighten the tension of the occasion. But it also appears twice in Paul's Epistles, when our rebirth as children of God is being emphasized. 'You did not receive a spirit of slavery to fall back into fear, but you have received a spirit of adoption. When we cry, "Abba, Father!", it is that very Spirit bearing witness with our spirit that we are children of God' (Rom. 8:14–16); and similarly, 'And because you are children, God has set the Spirit of his Son into our hearts, crying, "Abba! Father!"' (Gal. 4:6). The repetition of the expression 'Abba, Father' in these two passages could possibly refer to some kind of code expression for the use of the Lord's Prayer, though that is debatable, since it does not appear in any of the Epistles. Whatever the precise reason or reasons for using the Aramaic 'Abba' alongside the Greek word for father, we can conclude that it was deliberate, perhaps echoing a memory of Jesus himself using the term in overheard prayer.

*        *        *

We have this strange word, Abba, and we may well ask why we should expect to use it of God in the first place? It expresses parenthood, and yet we could quickly say that motherhood is part of the process as well. In one of the new eucharistic prayers, the expression 'as a mother tenderly gathers her children you embraced a people as your own'[2] appears as a deliberate echo of two biblical quotations. One is from the prophet Isaiah: 'As a mother comforts her child, so shall I comfort you' (Isa. 66:13); and the other is when Jesus says of the people of Jerusalem: 'how often have I desired to gather your children together as a hen gathers her brood under her wings' (Matt. 23:37). Prayer to God as mother has good medieval precedent, as we know from the writings of St Anselm, in the eleventh century, and Mother Julian of Norwich, in the fourteenth, and it is good that the mother image has been recovered in the memory of the Church, to work alongside – and to complement – the image of father. Some, of course, have difficulties with father language in principle, either because they never knew their father, or because their memories are so distorted and difficult that the very mention of the name runs the risk of reawakening painful experiences. This problem was recognized by an eighteenth-century writer, William West, who wrote in a somewhat pragmatic but perceptive vein that 'in the first place, we should be very careful not to ascribe any of the imperfections or weaknesses of earthly parents to God our Heavenly Father, who is infinitely above them.'[3]

We *have* to describe God somehow! And when we do so, we begin to realise that all forms of address to God are analogical, which means that we are using human language, but not in exactly human ways. To call God 'Father', in that intimate but respectful way, is to say that he is like a father, but he is so much more. We can also look at other ways in which we might describe God, but none of them quite has the resonance and richness of 'Father'. 'Lord' is about power. 'Creator' is about the mechanisms of the universe. And if we look further at the Lord's Prayer, we can identify five others. King – 'your kingdom come.' Leader – 'your will be done on earth as in heaven.' Provider – 'give us today our daily bread.' Forgiver – 'forgive us our sins as we forgive those who sin against us.' Protector – 'lead us not into temptation but deliver us from evil.'

We therefore come back to fatherhood, because it is profoundly relational. We are children, not rebels, nor slaves, nor servants. We are children of this heavenly father. We describe him in those terms as an act of trust on our part, but also recognizing the dignity that we have, as those who are reborn in Baptism, reborn from our natural existence; and that includes all the natural relationships that we have around us, whoever our parents are or were, and whether they have happened to have been any good at parenting. (As a wise priest once said to me when my children were young, 'We are all bad parents in one way or another!') This is why St Paul takes pains to point out that we are *adopted* by God, hence our privileged position in being able to call him 'Abba, Father' (Rom. 8:15; Gal. 4:7).

The spirit of adoption means that we are adopted by God, an experience which naturally adopted children know to be sometimes strange and not always easy.

We do indeed have to find some way of describing God, in order to address him in prayer, and the New Testament favours father. In the fourth Gospel, Jesus speaks of the 'Father' no fewer than seventy-five times, and the First Epistle of John uses it twelve times. By contrast, in Luke's Gospel, Jesus uses the term 'Father' five times, and in Matthew he uses it twice, but 'my Father' three times. This may well reflect the Aramaic language, where 'my' is never added to 'Abba', but merely implied to be there. On the other hand, the expression 'your Father' occurs only once in John's Gospel (John 20:17) but it appears in Luke three times, and twelve times in Matthew, where in all but four passages the expression 'heavenly' or 'in heaven' is added.

*     *     *

Why, then, the apparent addition of 'our' and 'in heaven'? Neither of these appears in Luke's version of the prayer (Luke 11:2) but that is not necessarily an argument against them. In fact, both these additions add a great deal to the way in which the fatherhood of God is understood. At the most basic level, they point up both the intimacy ('our') and the distance ('in heaven') of that divine fatherhood. They may or may not have been part of the 'original' version of the prayer, if we are to take a more sceptical view about the authenticity of what we have before us in the Gospels, where it is Matthew's version but not Luke's. The expression 'Our Father' appears at the beginning of a eucharistic prayer in the *Didache*, the early Church Order: 'We give thanks to you, Our Father, for the Holy Vine of your servant, David, which you made known to us through your servant Jesus: glory to you for evermore' (*Didache* 9:1). And in the previous chapter of the *Didache*, there is a version of the Lord's Prayer very close to that of Matthew's text (*Didache* 8:2).

Many writers across the centuries have been quick to point out that the 'our' establishes from the beginning that the prayer is not an individual exercise, even though it may be recited by someone on their own. It begins with a bold statement that the fatherhood of God is something shared, and shared by all who dare to call upon his Name. Such a fatherhood is shared because it is imparted by the very nature of God himself. St Bonaventure (c.1217–74) was an Italian who joined the relatively new Franciscan Order, eventually becoming its Minister General in 1257. He began teaching publicly in 1248, and it is from around that time that he wrote a concise exposition of the Lord's Prayer for Franciscan preachers, in which he writes of the fatherhood of God: 'He is father firstly through the image stamped on us; secondly through the likeness pledged in grace; and thirdly through his eternal origin.'[4] We bear his image, we have his likeness, but he is the source of our being.

The 'our' aspect of that fatherhood, therefore, is about the nature of God himself, the starting point being his generosity alone, and not about our perceptions, which are necessarily partial. If we were to pray 'my Father in heaven', we would have to go on and pray in a self-centred vein, 'give me today my daily bread, and forgive me my sins', necessarily omitting any dimension of mutual forgiveness! While the ancient Latin and Greek religions referred to Zeus and Jupiter as father, the God that Jesus comes to show us has a fatherhood based on the fact that he is the one and only God, and we are his adopted children as this prayer teaches. The Psalter is perhaps one of the most supreme embodiments of Jewish piety, yet not one of the Psalms addresses God as father. But in the Gospels Jesus tells us that we can, and does so by example.

The 'our' is a mark (almost a prayer) of charity, which recognizes that we are not in the business of 'me and my Lord', interiorizing our religion, at the expense of our relationships with other people – and at every level. It is easy to retreat into that individualistic world and make oneself both invulnerable and infallible. But to live the gospel of the fatherhood of God is about being vulnerable and fallible; it is about being open to other people, both those who openly share the fatherhood of God and confess the Christian religion, and those who do not and may be hostile. Indeed, the very anonymity of the community that recites this prayer (Jesus doesn't define it either in individual, national, or religious terms) makes it necessarily open-ended. It means, too, that when I open my Office Book to say Morning Prayer when I am on my own, the last thing that I would ever think of doing is to say 'O Lord open *my* lips', because I am taking part in the prayer of the Church, not in isolation.

Matthew also includes 'in heaven'. He describes God as 'your heavenly father' no fewer than three times in the Sermon on the Mount immediately after giving the Lord's Prayer (Matt. 6:14,26,32). This provides an essential contrast with our earthly father, whatever he may have been like. It adds, too, a contrast with our earthly mother, whatever she may have been like. And it adds a contrast with a false worldliness, which might try to turn Christianity into such an earthly business that it is of no heavenly use. But why 'in heaven' and not 'heavenly'? There is a small translation question surrounding 'in heaven'. Aramaic does not know the adjectival form, 'heavenly', which probably explains why the original Greek version, carried over into Greek liturgical use to this day, has the expression which is best translated as something like, 'Our Father who (is) in the heavens'.

But what is heaven? John Sweet describes heaven as the place 'where past, present and future exist as one whole'.[5] It is a nonspatial place, a reality which we are able to glimpse through the words and work of Christ. This means that our lives here on earth, as his younger brothers, know and experience what heaven will be like, in sharing that divine fatherhood, when we call upon his Name, and live a life of costly discipleship. Matthew, who provides us with this heavenly point of reference, in like manner ends his Gospel with Jesus' parting words to the disciples: 'All authority in heaven and on earth has been given to me' (Matt. 28:18). 'In' and 'on' have different resonances; to be '*in*' heaven' is more permanent and lasting than to be merely '*on* earth', and that is a gospel statement in itself.

Thomas Becon (1512–67), one of the early English Reformers, was for a time Chaplain to Archbishop Thomas Cranmer. He wrote a catechism which includes a lengthy section on prayer. This is how he describes the fatherhood of God:

How cometh it to pass, that God is our Father, seeing that we are flesh and blood, corruption and dust? God is our Father two manner of ways: first, in that he hath created and made us; secondly, in that he hath begotten us anew, not of mortal, but of immortal seed, in that he hath given us his Spirit, and we believe in his Son Christ Jesu.[6]

# Hallowed Be Your Name

To each one of us, our names are special. We may not have had much to do with how they were given to us. The Christian name is given at birth, and it is a sign of our identity from earliest childhood onwards. There are occasions, however, when people assume another name, for example at Confirmation, or when making a religious profession. I was given my name at Baptism and it wasn't until later that I discovered that the name Kenneth means leader. There are meanings to most names, so that David means beloved and Elisabeth probably means dedicated to God. We all grew up with our names, and they become so familiar to us that we sometimes forget what they are. They become sounds that indicate who we are. And then there are occasions when we suddenly wake up to the fact that they are more than that – because they are about *us*.

When we come to say the words 'hallowed be your name', however, we are moving to different territory. We know what our own names are, and it is to us that God has given the task of naming every creature on earth, animal, vegetable and mineral (Gen. 1:26ff). It is, at one level, an essential way of communicating, so that we know what things are called, whether it is a cauliflower, a dog, or a particular constellation in the heavens. There is, therefore, an element of control in this process, just as is suggested in the passage in Genesis. When, for example, immediately after the giving of the Lord's Prayer in Luke's Gospel, Jesus speaks about the friend who asks for three loaves at midnight (Luke 11:5), we know exactly what three loaves means, because bread is bread. We could not exist as a society without the means of description. Description means, therefore, not only individuality (a person) but category (a desk as opposed to a bookshelf).

But how do we describe the name of God? The simple answer is that it is impossible! When Moses had his vision of God in the burning bush (Exod. 3:1ff), he was called to lead the people of Israel out of slavery into the promised land, and he naturally asked who he should say had given this command. God replies, after some pressure, 'I am who I am' (Exod. 3:14). This is a description that people have pored over for centuries and have never entirely understood, because God is indescribable. But as the one who 'is who he is', God is the one who is, who was, and who is to come (Rev. 4:8). 'I am who I am' – this is a barely utterable expression, and one that devout Jews refuse to say.

\* \* \*

And yet we have to give God a name – but a name that does not turn him into an idol, something less than himself, nor a name that suggests that we are somehow in control of him. That is why the God 'who is' is to be 'hallowed'. In this 'hallowing' we are led again back to the scene of Moses in the desert, where God tells Moses to remove his shoes from his feet, because the ground on which he is standing is holy (Exod. 3:5). There are many different ideas of what is holy but whenever we do refer to holiness, we mean by the term a quality that suggests both difference and distance. The holiness of God makes us conscious of how different and distant we are from him, because we cannot describe him, at least not in ordinary terms. And whenever we try, we know that, even in terms like 'Father' – 'Our Father' – they are not fully adequate. Ernst Lohmeyer (1890–1946), one of the leading Lutheran New Testament scholars of his generation, disappeared after the Second World War at the hands of the Soviet invaders, having been part of the German Church struggle against Hitler. In his remarkable study of the Lord's Prayer, which was first published in German after his death in 1952, and then appeared in English translation in 1965, he writes as follows:

This is the essential link about the concept of holiness, that binds God and man together in one communion. It is not a principle of separation but of conjunction, not the idea of a basic distinction but the establishment of a basic communion. The only difference between God's holiness and man's holiness is that God *is* holy, whereas men and nations *become* holy.[1]

God's holiness, therefore, is essentially about his nature, which means to desire the re-establishment of our communion with him – hence that telling statement that whereas God *is* holy, human beings and nations *become* holy. As human beings, we are not upstarts before God trying to be God, but nor are we worthless and grovelling creatures fit only for destruction. We *can* share in that holiness, that otherness. And this is why without holiness the Christian vocabulary is essentially incomplete. In fact, we could even go so far as to say that each ingredient of the Christian vocabulary and experience is taken over from everyday usage and given new meanings – that is, with the exception of holiness. We can talk of Baptism, which means to wash. We can talk about redemption, a metaphor from the slave market, to express the way in which our freedom from sin has been bought by God. We can talk about liturgical vesture, and then realise that it was all originally ordinary forms of clothing; the Latin texts of the Roman rite have usually referred to the cope as 'pluviale' – a raincoat.

All these aspects of Christian vocabulary and experience have, to a greater or lesser extent, been 'baptized'. They have been taken over and given a new use and a new meaning. They have been 'made holy'. But that implies that there is something called holiness, something about being holy, which is something else altogether. We call these terms like redemption and these ritual actions like Communion 'holy' because they are ways of expressing that sharing in the divine life which God yearns us to have and to know (2 Pet. 1:4). So the holiness of God is different. The old English word 'hallow' is the same word that was used for saint, just as the Greek word 'hagios' is used both for the holiness of God and of the saints of the Christian calendar. Indeed, in the Eucharist, we speak of these 'holy gifts' precisely because, although the bread and the wine remain in scientific terms bread and wine, they become heavenly, after a spiritual manner, and are therefore set apart from all profane use.

In all the Greek liturgies since the fourth century, there has been a kind of liturgical argument immediately before Communion, in which the president says 'holy things for holy persons', to which the reply comes, 'one is the holy, one is the Lord . . .'.[2] That argument states the obvious Christian truth – the 'and yet' of Christian faith – that the great and holy God is prepared to stoop to earth, in his Son Jesus Christ, in order to feed his people in the bread and wine of the heavenly meal. The same paradox is expressed, less forcefully, in the Scottish Liturgy of 1929, where in the Consecration Prayer the Holy Spirit is invoked upon the gifts of bread and wine, 'that being blessed and hallowed by his life-giving power, they may become the body and blood of thy most dearly beloved son, to the end that all who shall receive the same may be sanctified both in body and soul, and preserved unto everlasting life.' And later, in the bidding after Communion, there is a direct reference to those who have received Communion as 'being made holy'.[3]

There are different words that have been used to translate this process of hallowing. In his study of the Lord's Prayer, William Barclay (1907–78) mentions several translations some of which use the word 'hallowed'; others use the word 'holy'; others again, 'sanctified', and yet others use the word 'revered'.[4] The word in the Greek – 'hagiazō' – is very rare in the New Testament, and unknown in ordinary secular Greek. And that proves the point of this petition in the Lord's Prayer. It is essential, near the start, to establish the otherness of the nature of God. It is right to begin with the eternal Father, creator and redeemer, who is both 'our' and intimate, but who is also 'heavenly' and distant. The petition 'hallowed be your name' follows from that description of the Father's presence 'in heaven'. Indeed, that holiness of God which reaches from heaven to earth is expressed perhaps at its most solemn and sublime in the *Sanctus*, the hymn, 'Holy, holy, holy . . .', which has for centuries been an essential part of the Eucharistic Prayer, because the Eucharist is the heavenly table on earth. As Bryan Spinks (1950– ) writes:

> In Christ the space of heaven and the region of the earth are united. In the eucharist the worshipper enters heaven through Christ, and is represented by our true High Priest. Here time and eternity intercept and become one, and this world and the world to come elide.[5]

The Lord's Prayer begins with those relatively easy words, 'Our Father in heaven'. But it continues in a more mysterious, different and distant realm, by using words that take us beyond ourselves. We move, therefore, into the totally indescribable, and yet that has to be put into words. God's name is . . . well, I can't quite put it into words . . . he *is* our Father, and yet he is in heaven . . . and he is and does many other things, but, again, I can't quite put it into words . . . But I know that I have to try, and yet the more I try, the more useless I find my own words, . . . which leaves me saying that . . . God simply *is* and there is not much that I can do about it, except respond to the fact that God is, and that I find God, him, or her, or it, or however I can possibly describe God's self . . . as the only viable explanation of the world that is about me, the experiences that I have in my life, and those handed on to me by others. God is, therefore, *holy* – utterly other, however intimate and personal I know him in Jesus Christ.

\*    \*    \*

And that brings us to the word 'be'. 'Hallowed *be* your name.' It is a neat little word, a request for something to keep happening, which is the meaning of the original Greek. The same desire to keep happening recurs in the following two petitions 'your kingdom come' and 'your will be done on earth as in heaven'.

The mood of the verb only changes into a polite order – the imperative as it is called – in the second part of the prayer, when we come to our own recurring needs, 'give us', 'forgive us', and 'lead us not . . . but deliver us . . .'. But who is doing the hallowing? It is us but it is not. Only God can do the hallowing. But we can also be 'mini-hallowers', as people who co-operate – however fitfully – in the work of God himself. *We* respond to the difference and distance of God, by praying that *we* may hallow his name, may recognize his existence, may respond to his love, may share in his nature, by the sheer fact that Jesus, and Jesus alone, into whose name as saviour we have been baptized, bridges this difference and distance, by showing us the human face of God. Perhaps, as Martin Kitchen once remarked, 'We hallow what we cannot handle.'

We are face to face with the baptismal character of the Lord's Prayer. Matthew's Gospel, in which the Lord's Prayer figures as such a prominent part of the Sermon on the Mount, ends with Christ's command: 'Go therefore and make disciples of all nations, baptizing them in the name of the Father and of the Son and of the Holy Spirit, and teaching them to obey everything that I have commanded you. And remember, I am with you always, to the end of the age' (Matt. 28:18–20). The urgency of the Christian mission is similarly taken up by Peter Abelard (1097–1142/3) in his exposition of the Lord's Prayer when he writes: 'All the scriptures shout out and all resound that "your name is holy". The name of the Lord, my brothers, is indeed holy, but it can still be made more fully holy in the hearts of people.' And he goes on to list, in a style characteristic of his time, pagans, Jews, false Christians, and – last of all – Christians themselves, who need to grow more fully in the faith. 'The more perfectly somebody believes and loves God, the more fully does he sanctify himself the name of God and show himself sanctified.'[6]

# Your Kingdom Come

There are two ways of describing a monarch. The most common is to describe them as either a king or a queen of a geographical country, like Sweden or Holland. But there is an older and less common way, which instead refers to the people. We still speak of 'Mary Queen of Scots' or more recently of 'Constantine, the King of the Hellenes', meaning the Greeks. The fact that there are these two ways suggests an uncertainty about kingship in relation to countries or peoples. This is nothing new. Nationhood is about what state we belong to. Ethnicity is about what tribe we belong to. And the history of human civilization has been one long tale of different nations and ethnic groups buffeting each other for power, whether that power is expressed in political or economic domination. Once one particular nation or ethnic group becomes dominant, others may gang up against it, as happened, for example, in the collapse of the Roman Empire. And students of cultural history know that the most assertive episodes have a habit of collapsing in tragic circumstances, as happened at the end of the Second World War in Germany.[1]

In our own time, we have come to see the state as a provider of all that we want or need. We pay taxes in order to have certain rights from the state and these provide us with assumptions about the economics of everyday life which may privilege one nation over another. This may lead into difficulties, such as has happened in Britain's National Health Service that requires a far greater subsidy with an ageing population and an increasingly complex medical technology as compared with the simpler social context after 1945 when it was established. New opportunities inevitably produce new problems. And one of these problems today, it would seem, is the need for people to feel and express their sense of *belonging*, as active citizens, taking part in every aspect of our common life, rather than as passive recipients, always looking for our rights.

When we come to the New Testament, it is clear from the start that the kingdom – the kingship – of God is about neither a geographical country nor a particular race. Nor is it about passive recipients and their rights. It is – in every sense – about *belonging*, and belonging to a project that is always on the way, and which at every level combines affection with demand. It is a kingdom, a kingship, which is about that paradoxical nature and name of God, who is both infinitely unknown and blatantly obvious, who is both accessible in every way and yet deeply mysterious. We keep living with the consequences; and the consequences are that the kingdom, the kingship, is preached and inaugurated, but it is always on the way.[2]

This kingdom does not settle on boundaries that we ourselves make, whether of geography or race. Nor does it settle on a particular version of the Christian faith, as if we have the right to exclude others who do not happen to agree with us. There are sometimes unattractive signs of that exclusiveness in the Church in every age. Nor is it about a sentimental vagueness which does not require us to believe – or to think – anything specific at all, except to try to be nice. Nor again is the kingship of God tangible in the sense of being fulfilled and realised in our midst. It is infuriating and tantalizing because at one level it never seems to get going and happen and do something! But it is in another sense something so profound and real that we cannot escape its truth. When we read of the kingdom of God in the Gospels of Mark or Luke, or the kingdom of heaven, as it is usually called in Matthew's Gospel, we are confronted with the fact that Jesus is the kingdom, and that all that he does and says – whether we understand it or not – expresses that kingdom. But because Jesus does not force himself on us, either by domination or manipulation, but leaves it to our choice, this kingdom is always going to be on the way, and it is never going to be completed by us.

It is important that we grasp this truth about the Christian gospel, particularly at a time when there is a great deal of rhetoric about the need for mission and evangelism – and rightly so. We are not here to push the kingdom of God onto other people, and adopt a method of mission and evangelism from the past. But neither are we here to 'sell' the good news, as if it were a commodity to manipulate people into buying. There will always be unfinished business about this kingdom, and those who try it out are going to be disappointed if they think that it will solve all their problems. There is no easy answer to the question 'How do I evangelize?' in a society that is over-cynical about people trying to sell things, but at the same time shows signs of astonishing credulity in the face of advertising.

Jesus leaves the kingdom to our choice. And that leaves us looking for the signs of its dawning, which we will glimpse here and there: unforgettable private moments, like comfort and sorrow; and social judgements, like the abolition of slavery. But we have enough behind us of the memory of Jesus, and the power of his presence among us in the Holy Spirit, to walk through this life in the belief that we can know heaven now. This kingdom is about both contemplation and action. It is not a question of 'either/or': it is 'both/and'. In Luke's Gospel, the Lord's Prayer comes sandwiched between Mary at Jesus' feet and the friend asking for bread at midnight (Luke 10:38–11:8). Those who want to stay with Mary by Jesus for ever find he has moved on elsewhere, and will easily forget to give bread to others; and those who are so intent on distributing food to the poor and little else will forget that they, too, need to gaze on Christ in worship. Discipleship is about listening generously to Jesus when we need to, as well as the call to give generously to others when they are in need themselves.

We keep being drawn back into that 'kingdom' – that life which calls us to worship and wait upon God. It can be its own challenge, particularly in a world like ours which often gives the impression of having no time for useless activity such as worship, except when the consumer need arises, such as a time of personal or family or community crisis. Of course the kingdom of God in its visible and deeply fallible form – the Church – needs to be there at those moments, but it is about more than rescue, comfort and help. It is the kingdom that Christ comes to embody, to spread a spiritual canopy, a frame of reference, in the *daily* needs of fellow human beings when these confront us, whether or not they are thought to have the right to claim our attention. There is an *embodied* character to the Christian faith. It is not about a worthy spiritual journey inwards to an autonomous 'me', but rather about ourselves in relation to God, other people, the world.

\*   \*   \*

Much of what we pray in the Lord's Prayer has echoes in the Old Testament: the heavenly Father, the hallowing of the name, the doing of his will, bread in the wilderness, mutual forgiveness, and divine protection along the way. But this particular petition – 'your kingdom come' – is without parallel.[3] Yet it is truly at the very heart of the Lord's Prayer. We are not waiting passively, shrugging our shoulders at the inevitability of everything around us. Or perhaps we are? I once had a conversation with someone in one of the caring professions who was beginning to think about retirement. After a few moments, he looked sadly at me and said, 'But you clergy go on until you are sixty-five, and you can, because you believe in what you are doing, and you still have faith.' I do not know whether I always believe in everything that I do! What I do believe is that we are *all* called to believe in the realities of things that are far beyond surviving the next budget cut, making the most of that cheap offer there, or arguing yet again for the retention of that particular post which is under threat. If our sights are set low to mere survival in a secular world, colluding totally with its specific (and at times intolerant) dimensions, we are never going to be able to see any signs of the kingdom of God, in judgement, mercy, love, forgiveness, generosity, or self-sacrifice.

To pray 'your kingdom come' brings us into the tension that this man Jesus has left as an indelible mark on human history. It is not my kingdom, or my version of what he said or did, or what I might think he should do now, or my private desire for him to 'listen' cosily to my needs, in isolation from others. It is *God's* kingdom, God's reign, not over a country or a group of people or a particular church, but over the whole of human history. It is a kingdom that affirms what is good and true and just in every age, just as it corrects what is misguided and unjust and wrong. It is a kingdom that can absorb the whole scene, and somehow make sense of it. The petition 'your kingdom come' is a prayer about obedience – attending to – God in His mission. And that is why the 'listening' must be about ourselves listening to God.

This kingdom is not a political or a national kingdom, but a community which, under God's care, lives its life in love and joy and peace. As Lohmeyer says, writing under the shadow of Hitler's Germany, 'There is room for a completely new order.'[4] And the kingdom is never far away, as the New Testament repeatedly tells us. Mark's Gospel, the briefest and the most abrupt of all four, begins with Jesus' Baptism, continues with the calling of the disciples, and then proceeds immediately with the healing in the Capernaum synagogue of a man with an unclean spirit (Mark 1–3). The secret of the kingdom is given to the disciples (Mark 4:11) and later in the same chapter, Jesus likens the kingdom to someone who scatters seed on the ground (Mark 4:26).

In the limited dimensions of human history, it is still a kingdom that cannot be shaken (Heb. 12:27). And it is a kingdom that starts with an invitation, includes repentance, is about ourselves, but is always about other people – and it is never far from us. This may explain why the two categories of people in the Beatitudes at the start of the Sermon on the Mount who possess the kingdom of heaven are 'the poor in spirit' and 'those who are persecuted for righteousness' sake' (Matt. 5:3,10). The kingdom of heaven is, therefore, not about the rich in spirit, or those who have an easy time. Heaven on earth reaches the very depths of human circumstances, whether we are apparently born to it ('poor in spirit'), or we are maltreated for it ('those who are persecuted for righteousness' sake'). There is a relent-lessness about that kingdom in its potential to reach the un-noticed, the undervalued, the ignored, and the deliberately put-down.

\* \* \*

This kingdom, therefore, is about much more than 'what's in it for me'. In faith, there are no guarantees, and it will not be possible for us to take God to court on the day of judgement for all the disappointments that he has given us, and for all the ways in which the fine print, that we ourselves impose on the Church and the Bible, has not somehow been met in full measure. In order to handle the 'now-ness' and the 'not-yet' of this kingdom, we can speak of the kingdom as we know it now, inaugurated by Christ, as 'the kingdom of grace', and the kingdom that will be finally revealed, and completed in Christ, as 'the kingdom of glory'.

In 1928, Pope Pius XI instituted the Feast of 'Christ the King' in the Roman Catholic Church, to be celebrated on the last Sunday of October. It was a bold gesture, given the political situation in Europe of his time, with the growth of fascism. After the Second Vatican Council, the feast was moved to the Sunday before Advent, to act as a kind of buffer between the end of one Christian year and the beginning of another. Other Christian traditions have followed this lead, and it adds an extra flavour to this part of the year. The kingdom of grace and the kingdom of glory flow from one to the other, and we are able to know the former all too well, in the hints and signs, the Word and Sacrament, as well as the poverty and pain of being a community of faith in human history. But the kingdom of glory is the horizon, the end point for which we yearn, when we ourselves – we hope and pray – will live to see past, present and future, gathered up into a perfect and energetic unity.

The twentieth century, which saw far more human suffering

than, it seems, any other, and many more Christian martyrs, by no coincidence saw also a recovery of the sense of the Eucharist as a looking forward to that kingdom, and there are indications of this in nearly every revision of the eucharistic liturgy in the Christian churches in recent decades. As Geoffrey Wainwright (1939– ) has eloquently put it: 'The eucharist proclaims that for men the kingdom of God means righteousness, peace and joy in openness to the divine presence, and already the Lord is establishing these things by His coming at the eucharist.'[5] Our response to the prayer for the kingdom is to live the life of the Beatitudes. Maximus the Confessor (c.580–662), one of the Eastern Fathers, brings us to the heart of this yearning:

If the indestructible might of the unfading kingdom is given to the humble and the meek, who would at this point be so deprived of love and desire for the divine gifts as not to tend as much as possible towards humility and meekness to become – to the extent that this is possible for man – the image of God's kingdom?[6]

# Your Will Be Done, on Earth As in Heaven

There is a tenseness about this petition that is unavoidable. It is easy to see why, for it is here that we encounter head-on the truth that 'prayer is both resting with God and wrestling with God.'[1] There is something of a contrast between the ills and the imperfections of this world, and the summing up of it all for which we pray through Christ in heaven itself. There can be no dispute about the unsatisfactoriness of this life, and though not everyone will agree in the reality of heaven, some hold on to it, even if in purely sentimental terms. We are told that many more people believe in heaven than think much of the Church, and this perhaps explains the sudden outpourings of grief when a famous person dies, and the often do-it-yourself approach to funeral services, where it is sometimes difficult for the priest concerned to inject a sense of the gospel as being about judgement and forgiveness, as well as invitation and joy.

Many people have not really thought about heaven at all. For the majority, I suspect, it is pushed into some kind of vague afterlife, which has little to do with what we are experiencing here on earth. That may well have been a central part of the quest for inquiring faith from the very first moment that a human being thought seriously about why they were there in the first place. It is, therefore, an essential background. But we need to press on and move further because if heaven has any reality at all, it must impinge on what we are doing here on earth. This, at any rate, is what the Christian faith keeps suggesting to us, not least through that elusive image of the

kingdom of God which is expressed in the petition 'your kingdom come'. The poetic is important, because it puts into words
what we cannot express in prose. But the poetic, in order to
have any real bite, has to express some kind of reality as well,
which is why we go straight on to pray, 'your will be done on
earth as in heaven'. Heaven is where past, present and future is
seen as one, through God's eyes. Earth, on the other hand, is
our perspective on our own present, informed (or otherwise) by
our knowledge of the past, and fed (or otherwise) on our hope
for the future. The extent to which we recognize the reality of
the present, instead of denying its existence by living a lie, and
the way we are prepared to learn from the past and live in hope
for the future – these are our main highways to heaven. We
walk there through the preacher of Nazareth, and his con-
tinuing significance for the human race.

Robert Leighton (1611–84), who was a central but in the end
unsuccessful reconciling influence in the seventeenth-century
Scottish Church, and who served for a time as Archbishop of
Glasgow, saw these tensions clearly. On the one hand, he says,
'The obedience of heaven is cheerful,' but he recognizes that
'answerably to the sense of this petition, do godly men, in
prayer, vent their regret and grief unto God, that there is so
little regard and obedience to His will amongst men.'[2] And as
one who lived through religious and political troubles at their
toughest (the Civil War, and the inability of presbyterian and
episcopalian parties to resolve their differences), Leighton the
pastoral scholar and peacemaker inwardly wept at the sheer
earthliness of the society and the Church he lived in.

It is not just the tension between earth and heaven. It is also
the tension of knowing what that will is – as Leighton and many
others have movingly commented. We speak of a 'battle of
wills' between people. This may be the tragedy of warfare
between neighbouring countries, often ethnically (or even reli-
giously) based. On the other hand, it could be the tension
between two people, two colleagues, or even husband and wife.
This may be creative; after all, the first promise made by
husband and wife at the marriage service consists of two words

– 'I will'. That word *will* has some emphasis about it, indicating a concentration of the will, through the whole personality. Sometimes the battle of wills takes the form of an argument between two groups. This may be encouraged by the environment in which the argument happens, as in the British Houses of Parliament, where Government and Opposition and other parties and groups face one another across an open space, rather than sit round in concentric circles, as in other modern democracies. The best moment that I think of in working closely with colleagues is when an idea that one person puts forward is explained and taken apart – in heart and mind – in order to clarify what the best course of action is likely to be. One prays for wisdom and courage, for maybe it is right to revisit that issue later, rather than take a snap decision. On the other hand, as many of us know, there can be the deliberate and uncreative kind of argument, arising out of a relationship that is not working which can often sour a marriage (when the conflict is between two partners) or a relationship at work (between two colleagues). There can be an intractable deathliness about those situations, for the creative spark has long gone, if it ever existed, and we are all the losers for it.

\* \* \*

Will suggests discovery, decisiveness, even assertiveness. Bishops, for example, are often asked to take a 'strong lead', except when the lead that they take happens not to coincide with the section of the ecclesiastical or social orchestra crying out for it. In discerning the will of God, a number of important factors have to be borne in mind. One factor is the words of scripture, and the values proclaimed by the very context in which Matthew gives us the Lord's Prayer, the Sermon on the Mount. Another is precedent, better called tradition, a living dynamic within the Church, and within other institutions as well. This is the distilled wisdom of how things have been done in the past, as well as what may or may not be possible and how mistakes have been avoided, and it provides a common block of collective experience by which we can interpret the present and dream about the future. Tradition can be oppressive. Good ideas can be blocked by the well-known time-serving adage that nothing must ever be done for the first time . . . And history is full of missed opportunities in this regard, like the reluctance of a Pope to send missionaries to China in the wake of Marco Polo's conviction that the terrain there was ripe for a new and fresh Christian presence.

This area becomes yet more personal when one considers St Paul at his more candid: 'For I do not do the good I want, but the evil I do not want is what I do. Now if I do what I do not want, it is no longer I that do it, but the sin that dwells within me' (Rom. 7:19–20). Here we have more than a hint of some-one who sees himself as an addict to sin, and who knows the need of forgiveness and of grace to lead him towards newness of life – which is why the Lord's Prayer moves on to pray for forgiveness and protection in its latter petitions. There is no point in preaching a Christianity that does not take what is sometimes called the human predicament in all its dimensions with the utmost seriousness.

Nor does God fail to take the human predicament with the utmost seriousness. For in all our weakness, we are still given rich capacities to learn from our mistakes, and to discover the meaning of love and self-sacrifice. The divine will and sacrifice are never far from each other, as Christian witness keeps reminding us. Michael Ramsey (1904–88), who kept returning to the theme of sacrifice throughout his writings, located it in the very heart of Christian living: 'where Christian people are themselves a sacrifice of praise, the divine voice is heard, and the world may begin to respond to its own true meaning.'[3]

It is in sacrifice, therefore, that we can find the basic touch-stone for discerning the will of God. Not a wet and fatalistic giving in to everyone else, nor the random surrender of princi-ple, but rather a determination to find where God can be found in the matters in hand. This may mean the articulate holding back in order to let the voiceless have a word; it may mean the powerful listening to the weak; and it may even mean hearing from somewhere the still small voice of calm (the 'sound of sheer silence' as the New Revised Standard Version translates it), rather than the wind, or the earthquake, or the fire – as Elijah discovered of old (1 Kings 19:11–13). There is much wind talked incessantly in a chattering generation, just as there is much earthquake, in the disturbance that we all experience through new projects, vision statements, and grand plans; and there is much fire, in the unleashing of new enthusiasms, as well as in the demolition jobs that can so easily be carried out on basic truths that the greatest minds and spirits of the past centuries have taken as read. But the still voice of calm, the sound of sheer silence? That emerges sometimes in self-sacrifice, nothing less.

\* \* \*

Earth may well give up on heaven, but heaven will never give up on earth. And here we are rescued from ourselves by the 'our' aspect of the Lord's Prayer. We are not on our own. We are not isolated and helpless cracked-up instruments of God's will, like a French horn with a hole in its brass tubing. We are collective enablers of that will to be done here and now, not in past generalities but in present realities. For the narratives of Jesus in the Gospels are not about that great plan that looks so slick and credible to the committee of inspection, but rather about chance meetings. The Gospels are indeed about a shapeless group of disciples around a wandering preacher who – strangely – betrayed not a hint of anxiety for the many hundreds of thousands of people he was *not* able to meet, *not* able to heal, *not* able to challenge.

Discovering the will of God does mean both resignation and positive action. We have echoes of both in the Gospels, particularly at that moment of testing for Jesus on the night of his arrest, a scene which has echoes, too, later on in the Lord's Prayer, when we pray not to be led into temptation itself. Mark's version of Jesus' prayer in Gethsemane ends with the words, 'Abba, Father, for you all things are possible; remove

this cup from me; yet, not what I want, but what you want'
(Mark 14:36). In Matthew, Jesus prays, 'My Father, if it is
possible, let this cup pass from me; yet not what I want
but what you want' (Matt. 26:39). Luke's version echoes
Matthew's: 'Father, if you are willing, remove this cup from
me; yet, not my will but yours be done' (Luke 22:42).

We need to pause here, because Luke has a slightly different
text: he prays simply 'Father', rather than 'my Father', as he
does at the start of his version of the Lord's Prayer (Luke 11:2).
But he omits this petition about the doing of the will altogether,
and yet he echoes it here more explicitly than Matthew, when
he prays, 'not my will but yours be done.' Why does Luke leave
out – or not have – this petition? Perhaps because it lies here in
Gethsemane, more directly than in Matthew's version. Perhaps,
too, because an earlier version of the Lord's Prayer could have
been shorter (though that is not necessarily the case). Perhaps,
also, because the doing of the will may have been interpreted by
him as synonymous with the coming of the kingdom. These are
questions which will continue to fascinate the scholars as well
as those many others who use these prayers. After all, Luke
omits the reference to the Father 'in heaven', so this petition for
the doing of the will on earth 'as in heaven' may have another
reason for not appearing here.

We are none the less left in Matthew – and in the standard
form of the prayer – with a petition for the doing of the will on
earth as in heaven immediately after praying for the coming of
the kingdom. And there is some good sense in it. The coming
of the kingdom is the coming of the kingdom of heaven. The
doing of the will draws us more explicitly into the picture, and
delivers the Christian response from being one of only word,
and not of deed. Matthew himself refers to doing 'the will of my
Father' as a prerequisite for entering the kingdom of heaven. It
is not about saying 'Lord, Lord' (Matt. 7:21) but whoever does
the will of the heavenly Father is 'my brother and sister and
mother' (Matt. 12:50).

Here is no clear-cut, impressive set of rules by which to live
which will be convincing to all-comers. 'There is a faith that

rebels and a faith that accepts, and they belong together.'[4] Grappling with the contradictions of human nature in our partial experience of the vision of God can indeed be a struggle, and anyone who gives the impression that it is all easy fails to face up to its true cost. Indeed, there are times when we only really know the will of God after we have done it. But the framework is none the less there, and we can call it by various names, including scripture, tradition and reason, already discernible between the lines of the New Testament. In 1717, a book was published called *A Collection of Meditations and Devotions* under another name, but written by a remarkable woman, Susanna Hopton (1627–1709). A pioneer of the place of women in the life and thinking of the Church, and as an equal (and not subjugated) partner in marriage, she wrote with passion and precision on this petition of the Lord's Prayer:

> O let me put to my seal, that God is true; let me subscribe to, and admire thy holy will. Grant my will may be in thine, and thine in mine, till they both become but one. If it be thy will to afflict me, thy will be done; to bereave me of my friends, or to let me enjoy them, thy will be done; to comfort or kill me, thy will be done. Grant me to be so assured of the goodness and perfection of thy will, that in all things it may be my desire that thy will be done.[5]

# 13

# Give Us Today Our Daily Bread

I can still remember places I have been to when the bread has come straight from the oven. I can think of the old village mill near where I was brought up in East Lothian. I can think of an upmarket bakery in a Manchester suburb. Or I can think of the shop in the medieval town of San Gimignano, in Italy, which I visited once on a holiday as a boy, where there was the added delight of knowing that the product emerged from an oven that had been there for centuries.

Bread is ordinary food, ordinary sustenance, ordinary provisions. In fact, the word for bread in Greek was often taken to mean any kind of ordinary fare, not necessarily bread made from baked wheat and yeast. It was this kind of bread that the people of Israel yearned for in the wilderness, when God responded by raining down manna upon them from heaven (Exod. 16:15). The difference there was that the Israelites did not know what this food was, hence the name they gave to it – manna – which is the Hebrew for 'what's this?'. In those unique circumstances, daily food was provided, and the people consumed it on a daily basis, because the ordinary ingredients for them to bake their own bread, their own food, were not available. And it is no surprise that after Jesus fed the five thousand in the wilderness, the Jews referred to eating manna in the wilderness (John 6:31,49). Jesus responds by using *his* provision of enough bread to feed a multitude and *himself* as the bread of life (John 6:35) to be an example of a new kind of manna, a bread that is both tangible and intangible, food for soul and body. Characteristically, John's Gospel, which has more extended teaching than the other evangelists, is the only one to have a discussion about manna in the wilderness. Whereas John does not contain any version of the Lord's Prayer, the petition for daily bread is echoed in those telling words 'Sir, give us this bread always' (John 6:34), which immediately lead into Jesus' statement that he is indeed the bread of life, and that whoever comes to him will never be hungry, and whoever believes in him will never be thirsty (John 6:35).

We all need daily bread, even though some suffer from tragic illness that prevents them from wanting to eat at all, just as there are millions who are hungry each day. But we need more than the daily bread that will feed our bodies. That is why this ambiguous petition begins the second part of the Lord's Prayer, at that vital change of gear when the prayer addresses *our* needs, and moves from petitions for the hallowing of the name, the coming of the kingdom, and the doing of the will, to that imperative, 'give'. The feeding of the five thousand in the wilderness and the teaching which follows it address this statement about the character of Jesus' ministry. The fatherhood of God, the meaning of the kingdom, and the doing of the will – all these are about feeding both the body and the soul, and never one to the exclusion of the other. Bread was and is an integral part of daily life, staple and ordinary food. It was and is an integral part of Jewish life and worship. It is no surprise that the food and drink of the Eucharist should be bread and wine, ordinary commodities, not special fare of any kind. It is a classless meal which is so counter-cultural that it has the capacity to level all those who draw near with faith to receive the food and drink of new and unending life in Christ. Bread is food, whatever table it is that we attend. The Eucharist highlights the Christian faith's embrace of the physical and the spiritual together. It *is* food and drink, and it points us back to the daily, ordinary sustenance that we need, and forward and upward to the heavenly, eternal sustenance of Jesus' teaching. There is an inherent ambiguity about the New Testament's understanding of the character of this food which cannot be resolved, focused particularly in the feeding of the five thousand in the wilderness (John 6).

Like the crowd that followed Jesus, we find ourselves in the wilderness and we need food. That food is supplied, but all it does is to lead us further on to more questions about the meaning of the lives that we lead, questions which Jesus himself helps us both to pose and to answer. Bread indicates daily sustenance on a journey rather than a static existence about merely living and surviving. The change of gear at this stage in the Lord's Prayer means that God is our gracious provider, and points to our indebtedness to him, our dependence on him. The food is not ready-made, but is itself the result of growth and destruction in the process of baking, just as wine is itself the result of growth and destruction in the process of fermentation.[1] We do not ask for everything to be handed to us on a plate. We do not ask even for *fruit*, which, though grown (and not baked) is seasonal. We ask for the basic daily material from which our sustenance can be supplied. From these materials we are ourselves able to provide bread for the breakfast table, the lunch table, the dinner table, and the Table of the Lord. It is not a question of having a deep-freezer full of enough bread to last until the end of our lives. We may have to work machinery of that kind in order to survive collectively in a complex world. But none of that can obscure the need for bread to be baked, and placed before us, day by day, and when we have eaten it, we know we will need tomorrow's bread as well.

*   *   *

That word 'give' marks not only a change in gear. It is also something of a contrast with the Jewish blessings over bread, which always refer to the bread as already provided by the Lord God, the one who nourishes, echoed in the new Offertory Prayers, 'Blessed are you, Lord God of all creation'. Here, once again, we see a subtle change. Some ancient commentators leapt to apply it to the Eucharist, whether or not it was celebrated daily. Others, like Gregory of Nyssa (c.330–c.395), insisted that this was ordinary food, essential nourishment, reflecting his sensitivity to the needs of the poor.[2] There are many layers of meaning in the Lord's Prayer, which is inevitable in a prayer of such brevity. This leads us to the question of how this petition should be translated, for although it reads with apparent ease in English translation, whether one is using the Prayer Book or the modern translations, there are two problems.

The first concerns emphasis rather than substance. Matthew has 'give us today', whereas Luke has 'give us *each* day.' Luke's emphasis on 'daily' echoes his call the disciples to take up their cross daily (Luke 9:23). But the real question concerns the Greek word translated by the adjective 'daily' in relation to the bread, which is 'epiousios', a word which appears nowhere else. Ancient commentators have translated it as 'bread for essential being', following Jerome (c.324–420), who had a strong influence on the formation of an agreed Latin text of the Bible. Others have interpreted it as 'bread for the coming day', or else – looking forward – 'bread for the morrow', which is probably where the burden of scholarship now lies. Much debate has taken place around this question, and it could well be that the original word was lost, or else that it was coined by the evangelists themselves, as Origen once suggested.[3] Certainly in the Ancient Near East ordinary bread was baked each day because it would not keep. We need to remember, too, that the first three Gospels speak more about eating and drinking than we find anywhere in the Old Testament. Indeed, one cannot really pray Christ's words for daily bread without taking into account his almost reckless readiness to sit at table with sinners (Luke 7:36–50). It is often interpreted as a sign of the coming kingdom, and is a feature of the ministry of Jesus that is emphasized in Luke's Gospel.

Given the fact that the prayer for the coming of the kingdom is the least Jewish of the petitions in the Lord's Prayer, we could conclude that the adjective 'daily' in relation to the bread was used for the first time and coined specifically for that purpose, in order to see this bread as the bread of the coming kingdom. The kingdom is both now and not yet, it is a daily experience, and one that will go on tomorrow, and the day after, until the end of time. Moreover, since that daily feeding is for our bodies as well as our souls, it is about daily food, every time we read and preach the Word of God, and every time we celebrate the Lord's Supper. It could embrace every possible dimension of nourishment. Such nourishment means surprise, disturbance, even confrontation. We are led again to Luke's Gospel, when Jesus ate on the Sabbath with a leader of the Pharisees, commented adversely on precedence in the table plan, and went on to call for the need to invite the poor, the crippled, the lame, and the blind (Luke 14:1–14). On that occasion, when one of the dinner guests rejoined with the words 'Blessed is anyone who will eat bread in the kingdom of God!' (Luke 14:15), Jesus went straight into the story of those invited to a feast who then gave excuses, and the subsequent open invitation to the poor, the crippled, the blind, and the lame to come instead (Luke 14:16–24). The bread for which we pray is the bread of the kingdom in all its totality, physical, spiritual, unconventional, and therefore eucharistic in every possible sense.

\* \* \*

Every day is indeed a gift of God, and every good and perfect gift comes from God himself (Jas. 1:17). The petition for daily bread has the atmosphere of a walk of faith, which makes it impossible to be static about Jesus. Before giving the Lord's Prayer in the Sermon on the Mount, Jesus has already argued with the devil in the wilderness that we do not live by bread alone, but by every word that proceeds from the mouth of God (Matt. 4:14). That 'word' is not always reassuring, which is why this petition is not comfortable. To pray for bread in this way judges our own superfluity of food, our economic misuse of it, our inability in a so-called global economy to eliminate world hunger – which we ought to be able to achieve at the stroke of a pen, or the click of the computer, *if* we were really as in control of our lives as we make ourselves out to be. To pray for 'our' daily bread is therefore to be aware of those for whom every day is a struggle against hunger and disease. There are times when I have seen pictures of human disaster on the large scale – like the scenes on television after the flooding in Mozambique – when I found myself almost unable to pray that prayer and then eat any food without feeling privileged beyond what I deserve. I am part of a human race that talks so much about high-level communication but which cannot organize itself in such a basic way as to ensure that these tragic events either do not happen at all, or when they do, food arrives swiftly, in the context of an international economy characterized by mutual trust.

There is indeed an economic reality about prayer. When we pray with other people, our prayers become informed about those *with whom* we pray as well as those *for whom* we pray. And that can turn our words into action. The generosity of God compels us to confront our own lack of generosity towards others: we must provide those needed loaves baked that day and left over for the friend who knocks on the door at midnight (Luke 11:5–8). There are, too, moving stories about people in the concentration camps of the Second World War who found the petition for daily bread either impossible to say – or else so full of thanksgiving for the very fact of surviving another twenty-four hours that it was impossible to put into words. Bread is the food of the poor, it is not about luxury. Christ's presence amongst the poor ensures that the food of the Christian meal was bread, vegetarian-style, rather than meat, which in those days was usually available only for the wealthy, or else sold off as leftovers after temple sacrifice, with all the problems which this involved for Paul at Corinth (1 Cor. 8:1–13).[4]

When it comes to the Eucharist, there has long been a lively – and unresolved – discussion over what kind of bread should be used. Broadly speaking, the East uses ordinary bread, as in much of the Protestant West, whereas Roman Catholics, as well as many Anglicans and Lutherans, use wafer bread. Sometimes special bread is baked which even looks like some kind of a halfway house between the two. History does not produce easy answers. But perhaps this reflects the paradox at the heart of that word 'daily', and the application of that word 'bread', for the Eucharist lives a life between and among these dimensions of the earthly and the heavenly, the now and the not yet.

Similarly, there are questions surrounding the frequency of the Eucharist. It has sometimes been remarked that people are receiving Holy Communion with greater frequency nowadays than they have been since the earliest times. History does not give a ready answer. Some early commentators indeed applied the word daily to a daily celebration of the Eucharist. Others again have expressed their reverence towards the sacrament by infrequent reception, as in parts of the Scottish Highlands to this day. Lent has long been a solemn season, which enthused Christians at Rome to make provision in the lectionary for daily Eucharists, whereas in parts of the East it was explicitly forbidden, except on Saturdays and Sundays.[5] But however frequent or infrequent the Eucharist, when prayer is offered for 'daily bread' over the consecrated gifts, before receiving them, the faithful Christian thinks ahead to the next occasion of such feeding.

Daily bread involves cost. Charles de Foucauld (1858–1916) was one of the most extraordinary figures in French Catholicism of his time. An ex-cavalry officer, he became a Trappist monk, fascinated by the Middle East and Algeria. He settled in the remote Hoggar Mountains, living as a hermit who was admired as much by the French military as by the local Muslim communities. He attracted no followers in his lifetime (he was assassinated by Muslims), but the rules that he wrote for religious community life were subsequently taken up to form the backbone of the Little Brothers and Sisters of Jesus, communities who came to live among the poor. His all-embracing meditation on daily bread springs out of a rare poverty of body and spirit:

You desire me, O Lord, to look to you for my every need. And in looking to you, I know that you will provide me with bread to eat, clothes to wear, and a warm place to rest. But it is not only material bread which you provide; you give also spiritual bread. Whenever I eat the bread of Holy Communion, I am reminded that your Son gave his body to die on the cross, to give me spiritual food for all eternity. And in this phrase, I note that it is not 'me' for whom I pray, but 'us'. You do not want me ever to pray selfishly, but always to pray for others' needs, because only through such mutual charity do I become fit to receive the true bread of eternal life.[6]

# Forgive Us Our Sins As We Forgive Those Who Sin Against Us

There are many stories about forgiveness failed and forgiveness succeeded. I can think of people who have found it impossible to forgive, even after the passage of time. The wound can result from a number of factors, such as the wickedness – or the stupidity – of the other person or party. As human beings, we live with the individual as well as the collective consequences of being part of a fallen creation. This means that earthquakes and hot springs coexist with viruses and good health, and new technology with road accidents. Many people may find it difficult to use the language of a fallen creation, with its inevitable implications of imperfection, though they may arrive at its meaning in time. To speak of a fallen creation does not imply a belief that we are destined for the gutter. What it does imply, however, is that all that we are and see and do is shot through with tendencies to create as well as to destroy, and that makes the lives we lead a path of discernment, in which collective wisdom is high on the list.

Collective wisdom about forgiveness is not in short supply. Sometimes it takes some years before being able to say certain things to people, and the gift of time in forgiveness is important in this process. I have never subscribed to the view of 'forgive and forget', because it is impossible to forget something that is really important, whether it is pleasant or unpleasant. The memory is central – it is what we do with it that is crucial.[1] If we took seriously the Gospel command to forgive one another which follows so immediately on Matthew's version of the

Lord's Prayer (Matt. 6:14–15), then, hard as it sometimes is, when we pray the confession together at the Eucharist, we should at least pray for the gift of the *intention* to forgive the other person or party some time in the future. Some people cherish grudges, and that can either turn sour, so that reconciliation is impossible, or it can turn in the other direction, and become an endearing joke, which eventually leads to some kind of reconciliation.

Then there are occasions when we want to extract something more with the forgiveness, and I have come across occasions when money has come into the request. For people like that, forgiveness somehow has to be matched in deed as well as word, as if the new relationship cannot be established on its own. There *are* instances where some kind of reparation is appropriate, such as property or possessions seized during an invasion which ought to be given back. In a society that is so fearful of risk, there are signs that litigation is becoming too much of a habit. That in itself could be dealt with in time more easily were we not also a society that finds it increasingly difficult to deal with what Rowan Williams has recently described as remorse and shame. 'There is no hope without remorse . . . refusing remorse amounts to defining "real" selfhood out of both time and conversation.'[2] This inability to handle remorse and shame goes strangely hand in hand with public expressions of regret. But regret is not the same as penitence; in a post-Clinton world, regret is not enough. There is no doubt about the fact that we know forgiveness better when we have learnt what it means for ourselves, and that involves more than simply regret: it must include that further vital step, repentance itself.

Then there are those relationships which *have* been healed. Captor and captive meet years after a war – and become friends. There have been moving scenes of precisely that, when long after the event ageing former warriors, whose memories of events long ago are doubtless far more vivid than what happened to them the day before, can still take that step and say that the past is forgiven. Warring factions in a family can come together at a graveyard, perhaps fulfilling the wishes of the deceased, or at any rate determined to avoid the kind of scene that would never be forgotten in years to come. Sometimes that determination to 'stick together' represents what seems to be a pragmatic approach to past wrongs. No doubt there are marriages which in the past perhaps would have ended in the parting of the ways, but there are too many approaches to living together today, whether in marriage or not, in which the precondition is no more and no less than that they stay together so long as they fit together, after which whatever they meant to each other becomes discarded. Forgiveness is indeed about the past, but it is also about learning how to handle the future with a more open heart. To go on to pray – as the Lord's Prayer does – for protection against temptation is, in part, to pray about lessons we may have learnt about our past.

When we contemplate such a range of opportunities taken and failed, we begin to realise that life is not fair and that our temperaments and circumstances are going to vary. What I am suggesting is that the Christian interpretation of life, whatever these circumstances, means that God gives us the freedom to love, whatever happens. And that love, like the rest of our lives, is contextualized, and necessarily so. Our lives are – most of them – probably going to consist of a jumble of experiences in which we have either responded to that challenge immediately or belatedly, or we have failed somehow.

*        *        *

This is perhaps the reason why the prayer for forgiveness comes immediately after the prayer for bread. Having contemplated the generosity of God in providing for our basic material welfare, and doing so with hints of how that welfare finds expression in the Holy Communion, we now contemplate the generosity of God's *forgiveness*. The forgiveness that God gives and that we are required to give to each other is echoed more strongly in Mark's Gospel, where there is no text of the Lord's Prayer at all, when Jesus points out, 'Whenever you stand praying, forgive, if you have anything against anyone; so that your Father in heaven may also forgive you your trespasses' (Mark 11:25) The forgiveness of sins is part of the gospel, and it appears throughout the New Testament, either explicitly (Eph. 4:32), or by implication, for it is writ deep and large in Christ's life and teaching, and above all in the meaning of his death and resurrection. New life and forgiveness are part of the same picture. You cannot have resurrection without forgiveness.

But what is it, precisely, that the prayer asks should be forgiven? There are different words for 'sins' which have different images. Matthew's version is unambiguous and speaks of what is owed in terms of debts. We ask that our debts be set aside, just as we set aside the debts that are owed to us by others. And Matthew makes the assumption that these have indeed been forgiven – 'as we also *have* forgiven our debtors' (Matt. 6:12). Luke, on the other hand, possibly for reasons of linguistic variety, uses a different word. We ask to be forgiven our sins (literally, the things where we miss the mark – an image taken from archery), just as we set aside all who owe us debts (Luke 11:4). True to form, Matthew's style is more direct, whereas Luke's is more cultivated.

In the sixteenth century, the two main English translators adopted different words at this point. William Tyndale (1525) used the word 'trespass', with its overtones of invasion of space, whereas Miles Coverdale (1535) used the word 'debts' (taken over from the Latin 'debita'), with its overtones of money. Trespass and debt also meant sin both at the time and before, as Tyndale and Coverdale knew well. Modern versions, on the other hand, go for the more direct word – 'sins'. There is something of an irony here. We do not nowadays talk about trespassing very often, but we often speak of invasion of one's own personal space; and while we have a more economically-based approach to the way we talk and think than we used to, we do not so readily see sin as a 'debt'.

It is, however, more important to grasp the meaning of the Lord's Prayer than to be attached to one particular translation.

The word 'debt' in Hebrew has a long tradition of connoting sin, just as the word 'trespass' in sixteenth-century English could mean an offence. But language changes, and in a world in which the language of economics is so strong, debt immediately suggests something financial, but not necessarily something that is wrong; and the word 'trespass' long ago developed exclusively legal overtones. For a prayer that was originally couched in such simple terms, it is perhaps wiser to go for a simple word like 'sin', provided that we take on board its reality and its meaning.

As Lohmeyer remarks, 'the word "forgive" appeals to God's innermost being, the word "debt" to an outward burden.'[3] The reality and the meaning are that sin is part of life and is real. Its reality and meaning in relation to God is that he is ready to forgive, and to have our relationship with him – and each other – individually and collectively restored. The breakdown of human relationships is such a realistic issue for so many people that to talk about sin and forgiveness reaches new meanings when it is applied in this collective social way. Perhaps it was Jesus' emphasis on the *collective* understanding of sin and forgiveness that was the most really innovative. That word 'debt' needs to remain in the background, even if we do not use it in our modern translations. There is an inescapably financial aspect to this petition which could be put at its sharpest by suggesting that it is only when we ourselves are ready to *cancel* the debt that we know what forgiveness really is, as Peter Selby has forcibly argued in relation to international economics in general, and Third World Debt in particular.[4]

*        *        *

Sin is so much part of life and is so real that it needs to be recognized and not skimmed over, and public worship often has to carry a great deal here. For example, there is a tendency to treat public confession in Christian worship sometimes like a prelude to be gone through, and no more. In the recent liturgical tradition, Catholic and Protestant, there has been an understandable reaction against excessive penitence. But perhaps the pendulum can go too far in the other direction. In the *Common Worship* (2000) form of Eucharist in the Church of England, there is a fine alternative Confession. It is an instructive blending of the Jewish *Shema* (loving God and loving our neighbour), with a strong sense of time (past, present and future), and of social responsibility – doing justly, loving mercy, and walking humbly with God (Micah 6:8):

> Most merciful God,
> Father of our Lord Jesus Christ,
> we confess that we have sinned
> in thought, word and deed.
> We have not loved you with our whole heart.
> We have not loved our neighbours as ourselves.
> In your mercy
> forgive what we have been,
> help us to amend what we are,
> and direct what we shall be;
> that we may do justly,
> love mercy,
> and walk humbly with you, our God.[5]

Such a confession implies both the mutual and the social aspects of forgiveness that are inherent in the New Testament, and which are just as much part of the reality of the lives that we know as our expectation that God will indeed forgive us. In the Absolution which follows it, we hear of the gift of forgiveness to all who truly repent, the reality of God's mercy falling on the penitent, the free gift of pardon and freedom from all sins, the confirmation and strengthening in all goodness in the future, and the 'keeping' in life eternal. When we turn to the Lord's Prayer, this makes the petition for forgiveness probably the hardest part to pray seriously, because forgiveness for human beings is so often about our own timescale, about when we feel ready to bury the hatchet, and about when we realise that keeping up the feud is hindering the kingdom of God rather than helping it. As Oscar Cullmann (1902–99) has written:

The honesty of our prayer requires that we ourselves should stand in the sphere, in the 'field of force', of forgiveness. In that case, any human claim to God's free forgiveness is excluded. However, we ourselves stand outside this divine field of force unless we are also ready on our part always to forgive; unless we are, it is meaningless to utter this petition.[6]

Sentiments such as these have been made frequently before. John Chrysostom (c.347–407) refers to this petition more often than any other in his sermons, to the point of castigating those who, it would seem, conveniently omitted it as too uncomfortable. Augustine frequently preached on the Lord's Prayer, particularly to those about to be baptized, and on one occasion, he refers to 'the daily purification of this holy prayer', meaning that we are washed *once* in the waters of baptism, and we are washed *daily* when asking for forgiveness in the Lord's Prayer.[7] That is a high view indeed and it makes another close link between the Lord's Prayer and the sacraments of Baptism and Eucharist. It is also an argument for making more of exactly where and how the Lord's Prayer is recited, introduced and followed on in those two sacraments. But however well thought out the technical presentation, this particular part of the Lord's Prayer, with all its tender searchings of the human soul, is a prayer where God is more interested in the heart that thinks and feels the words than the voice that gives expression to them.

These home truths lie behind what St Benedict has to say about the recitation of the Lord's Prayer. Taking a leaf out of Matthew's Gospel, with its insistence on the need to forgive, Benedict directs the superior of the community to recite the Lord's Prayer alone at Morning and Evening Prayer:

Assuredly, the celebration of Lauds and Vespers must never pass by without the superior's reciting the entire Lord's Prayer at the end for all to hear, because thorns of contention are likely to spring up. Thus warned by the pledge they make to one another in the very words of this prayer: 'forgive us as we forgive' (Matt. 16:12), they may cleanse themselves of this kind of vice.[8]

# Lead Us Not into Temptation But Deliver Us from Evil

We all know what temptation and being tested is like. The temptation to refuse another's need. The temptation not to forgive, or not to accept forgiveness. The most helpful way of looking at temptation is in the ways we have been tested, as communities, even as civilizations, and what we ourselves have managed to learn through the process. Black South Africans were tested sorely during the time of apartheid and that has left a scar on South African history. The ambiguous results of imperial history have left their mark, for example on India, after the departure of the British. Like our inability to manage daily bread for the whole world, or the forgiveness of international debt, temptation brings us back to the fact that the world is not entirely satisfactory.

This particular petition raises two difficulties. The first is technical and concerns how we view the arrangement of the Lord's Prayer. Many commentators have separated the prayer against temptation and the prayer for protection against evil from each other. There are good grounds for doing this, but to separate them destroys the symmetry of the prayer, so that the threefold character of each part is removed. The sixteenth-century Reformer, John Calvin, took the view that the two are part of the same petition: 'Satan tempts, that he may destroy, condemn, confound, throw headlong; God, that by proving his people he may make trial of their sincerity, and by exercising their strength confirm it.'[1] And many commentators and expositors since have followed his lead.

The second difficulty is more complex and concerns translation. The contemporary international English version of the Lord's Prayer translates the first part of this petition as 'do not bring us to the time of trial.'[2] The reason for this is that temptation and trial are the same word in Greek and many rivers of ink have flowed from the pens of scholars on the precise nature of this testing, this trial. Temptation in the New Testament usually means to be tested. The Letter to the Hebrews concentrates on pointing to the human side of Christ when the author affirms that 'because he himself was tested by what he suffered, he is able to help those who are being tested' (Heb. 2:18). This is why so many of those who have written on this part of the Lord's Prayer have usually insisted that temptation is a normal part of life.

But how should it be translated?[3] 'Time of trial' suggests a particular kind of testing, the ultimate one, that of falling away from God at the last. And that indeed is one of its meanings, one among many. It certainly evokes the atmosphere of Christ in the Garden of Gethsemane: 'keep awake and pray that you may not come into the time of trial' (Mark 14:38). Many people have found themselves there in that garden at moments of severe crisis in their lives. There are some who by temperament and circumstance seem to live in a permanent Gethsemane, and while they may have special gifts, they can sometimes be rather difficult to live with! There are also those who suddenly find themselves confronted with a difficult decision, more difficult than anything they have faced before, and Gethsemane suddenly becomes an unexpected and unfamiliar reality to them.

C. F. D. Moule[4] examines some of the details of the New Testament debate surrounding this part of the prayer. What we are probably faced with is the transition of the prayer as used by early Christians expecting the coming of the kingdom and the trials and testings that this would involve. As the Church 'settled down' into history, the deliverance prayed for had to embrace deliverance *within* testing. This is tantamount to saying that to pray against temptation is a wish unfulfilled, because it has become absorbed into everyday experience and is no longer about the 'end'. The early Christians themselves continued to wrestle with its meaning. There was a North African strand of interpretation in the early centuries, backed up occasionally by alternative texts, which translated the prayer as 'do not let us be led into temptation', a tradition known to Tertullian, Cyprian, as well as Augustine himself, who, although he did not use it, was familiar with it. There were also versions, known in the Irish Gospel manuscripts, which defined the temptation in terms of 'what we cannot bear.'[5] That particular translation echoes St Paul himself: 'No testing has overtaken you that is not common to everyone. God is faithful, and he will not let you be tested beyond your strength, but with the testing he will also provide the way out so that you may be able to endure it' (1 Cor. 10:13).

\*     \*     \*

One resolution of this dilemma is to opt for as all-embracing a translation as possible and hold on to an understanding of God which safeguards his involvement in creation as well as his distance from it. We are back to 'Abba, Father,' who is both 'our' and yet is also 'in heaven'. It may well be that 'time of trial' is how the earliest Christians understood these words, if this is indeed the original form of the prayer. But just as 'daily bread' has come to embrace a range of different meanings of feeding, so this petition has to embrace different kinds of testing, and these include both the day-to-day testings and temptations that were mentioned earlier, and the last temptation of all, which is to fall away from God himself. 'Time of trial' as a translation is too focused and precise, and is insufficient to resonate with the many different interpretations that have been used in the past and continue to be experienced now.

The petition not to be led into temptation is a symptom of the character of the Lord's Prayer as a prayer in a fixed and brief form whose meanings and interpretations live within a certain frame of reference. In these terms, temptation has to include human experience of all kinds that we would rather avoid in the future, as well as that which we dread most of all, falling away from God. But the prayer must embrace both, and not the latter only. The sheer negativity of this prayer – 'lead us not' – marks it off as unique, since it points to a future which we fear. Daily bread is about the present, forgiveness is about the past; temptation and deliverance are about the future. That 'not' is strong and powerful, and its force is about us not being overwhelmed. In this connection, some words from Julian of Norwich (c.1342–c.1416), the great English mystic, in her *Revelations of Divine Love*, are apposite: 'This word, "thou shalt not be overcome", was said full sharply and full mightily, for sureness and comfort against all tribulations that may come. He said not "thou shalt not be troubled, thou shalt not be travailed, thou shalt not be distressed"; but he said "thou shalt not be overcome". It is God's will that we take heed to these words, and that we be ever mighty in faithful trust in weal and woe. For he loveth us and liketh us; and so willeth he that we love him and like him, and mightily trust in him. And all shall be well.'[6]

The Gethsemane answer, therefore, is that Christ is already with those in temptation, not resolving the dilemmas in a contrived way that will still the conscience momentarily, but present among those questions, those tensions, including the pain that will sometimes not go away. While God has no desire to 'lead us' in an irresponsible manner into moments of testing, we would not be human beings if we did not ask them not to happen. If we take the Bible seriously, we should not be surprised about temptation, particularly as it begins with a narrative about temptation itself, namely the creation of Adam and Eve, sin and fall and all that follows (Gen. 1–3). If we believe that the work of Christ is about restoring us, characterized in the Holy Saturday scene of Eastern iconography, the dragging of Adam and Eve up out of hell, then part of the Christian response is to expect temptation and testing, and to keep praying for deliverance *from* it, and preservation *within* it. Temptation and testing can take many forms. Those in which we ourselves retain a responsibility for our actions mean that we pray to *withstand* them. And those in which it seems that we can have no responsibility at all are those in which we pray to be *preserved*. People who have been tortured for their Christian faith or who have lived 'on the edge' of life know how the one can gradually lead into the other.

There are, too, temptations in religion, of which Jesus warns us in the Gospels, pitfalls into which the zealous believer easily slips. We can turn following Jesus into an impressive system, instead of a vulnerable and questioning community. We can become an exclusive club, intent on keeping out those who do not conform to our stereotypes and who do not echo our particular prejudices. We can become possessive about the sacraments and treat them as our own, instead of gateways to heaven. And we can become too comfortable with the culture we live in, affirming its inherent weaknesses, but failing to see in Jesus 'the Man for Others' a figure who will always be a bit of a stranger to any age.

\*　\*　\*

This somewhat dark petition, like all the others in the Lord's Prayer, tells us something about the nature of God and the freedom we are given. We have prayed for food and forgiveness. We now pray for protection from a God who will walk before us. And that is why, immediately after shrinking from any form of temptation, we ask to be delivered from evil. Here we can be enriched, rather than confused, by the fact that in New Testament Greek we read '*the* evil', whereas Latin, which has no word for 'the', translates it as 'deliver us from evil.' This leads to the inevitable question, is evil personal or impersonal?[7] We can project our own interpretations and write our own paraphrases of the Lord's Prayer. Many have done so before us. But here as elsewhere, the translation must be brief and all-embracing, otherwise it destroys the spirit of the prayer. Some speak readily of a personal evil, while others are equally quick to speak of it as a force; the result is the same, for evil is about division, destruction, dehumanizing. John Calvin sat lightly to the question of whether the evil mentioned here was personal or impersonal. To pray for deliverance from evil faces up to the dangers by which we are surrounded, whether we are struggling to reconcile two opposing parties, or on a long journey in a human-made machine, like an aircraft, where things might not be as safe as they should be. This prayer recognizes that human resources are, at the end of the day, inadequate to deal with all eventualities, however well organized we think they can be. This prayer, above all, moulds together our own fear of risk in the future ('lead us not into temptation') with the weakness and destructiveness that are part of our world ('but deliver us from evil'). But the God who goes before us, who is 'prevenient', is the one whose everlasting arms and mercy will always reach out to us.

What, then, of this 'evil'? It is only in Matthew's Gospel that we have the prayer for the deliverance from evil, and the devil is later described simply as 'the evil one' (Matt. 5:37). Jesus wandering in the wilderness and experiencing temptation and testing (Matt. 4:1–11; Luke 4:1–13) is a scene that could be described as two rabbis having a dispute with each other. But as with translating 'temptation', we cannot think ourselves back into the position of being contemporaries of Jesus. It is impossible for us not to pray for deliverance from evil without taking into account the full meaning of the cross, and how we view it in the various images we have inherited, whether conquest of evil, cosmic battle, cheating the devil, absorption of evil into good, example of humility eternally vindicated, and much else; the repertoire has not been exhausted.[8] To pray for deliverance from evil means, as Calvin saw so clearly, the destructive and uncreative aspects of this world with which we ourselves can so easily co-operate, however we may describe them.

No one who has been involved with the pastoral care of the deeply disturbed, on the one hand, or the care of those who have been affected by forms of black magic, on the other, is unaware of this real dimension to reality. To use traditional imagery, if Christ conquers evil, there is a sense in which we can see the consequences of evil all the more clearly in the light of the resurrection. In a course of lectures on the Catechism, Thomas Secker (1693–1768), Archbishop of Canterbury in the eighteenth century, recognizes that 'our tempers, our ages, our stations and employments in the world, be they ever so different, may each in their different ways, risk our innocence.'[9]

In Luke's version of the Lord's Prayer, there is no petition for deliverance from evil (Luke 11:4). This does not indicate an underemphasis of evil in his Gospel in any way. The two parts of the petition are clearly related and Matthew could have added the second part (Matt. 6:13) as a response to the early Church's growing need to pray for deliverance from evil, as the fear of apostasy under persecution grew. But from our different perspective we may well view it in a different way. This whole petition recognizes that the future is uncertain and that it is an act of faith, not planning, of trust, and not control. By looking into God's future, it recognizes too that the Christian life is about a future where God's name shall be hallowed, in his eternal kingdom, where his will is known, and where there will be enough bread and to spare, and forgiveness aplenty. That hope we cling on to, as we face the daily consequences of the dimensions of fallen time and space in which we find ourselves now. From Anglo-Saxon times, people have prayed for deliverance from all kinds of evil in the litany, a practice that continues to this day in the Anglican liturgical tradition:

From all evil and mischief;
from pride, vanity and hypocrisy;
from envy, hatred and malice;
and from all evil intent,
*Good Lord, deliver us.*

From sloth, worldliness and love of money;
from hardness of heart
and contempt for your word and your laws,
*Good Lord, deliver us*

From sins of body and mind;
from the deceits of the world, the flesh and the devil,
*Good Lord, deliver us.*

From famine and disaster;
from violence, murder and dying unprepared,
*Good Lord, deliver us.*

In all times of sorrow;
in all times of joy;
in the hour of death,
and at the day of judgement,
*Good Lord, deliver us.*

Tom Wright puts all these truths succinctly:

By giving us this prayer, Jesus invites us to walk ahead into
the darkness and discover that it, too, belongs to God.[10]

# For the Kingdom, the Power and the Glory Are Yours Now and For Ever. Amen

How should a prayer end? Jesus can be stern about people who heap up words upon words, or who make a show of their religion in public, as he makes clear in the Sermon on the Mount before giving us the Lord's Prayer (Matt. 6:1–8). But all forms of public speech need a conclusion. Early on, Christian prayers began to conclude with the words, 'through Jesus Christ our Lord . . .' This useful formula serves a double purpose. It acts as a kind of liturgical full stop. But it also states the belief that all our prayers are united with Christ's prayer at the Father's right hand in heaven (Heb. 7:23–5), which is a figurative way of saying that Jesus Christ is the link, the inseparable link, between ourselves and the reality and love of God.

The text of the Lord's Prayer and the New Testament, however, end without this ascription of kingdom and power and glory to God. Matthew simply ends with 'lead us not into temptation but deliver us from evil', and immediately goes into a short exhortation on the nature of forgiveness (Matt. 6:13–15). Luke, on the other hand, does not have 'but deliver us from evil' at all, and moves straight from the petition against temptation to a warning that when a friend comes at midnight for three loaves of bread, we should respond, and not be tempted to refuse (Luke 11:4–8). But as the Church prayed this prayer, it had to have an ending, which was added to later manuscripts of Matthew's Gospel from the fourth century onwards.[1] But not all liturgical texts of the Lord's Prayer included it. In the Roman Catholic Eucharist, as soon as the congregation has recited the words 'deliver us from evil', the priest adds a short prayer elaborating on that deliverance:

> Deliver us, Lord, from every evil, and grant us peace in our day. In your mercy keep us free from sin and protect us from all anxiety, as we wait in joyful hope for the coming of our Saviour Jesus Christ.

Only at this point does the congregation join in with the doxology. The same kind of interjection, followed by the doxology, is to be found in nearly all the Eastern Churches to this day, except the Orthodox. The difference is that the Roman Mass never had the doxology until the revised version in 1970, when it did so as an ecumenical gesture to the rest of the Church. But this only applies to the Eucharist; in all other services of the Roman liturgy, daily prayer included, the doxology is entirely absent. The Greek Orthodox, however, knows none of these complications, but – like most of the Protestant West – has the doxology as an integral part of the prayer, without any interjection by the priest and it is a common conclusion to other prayers as well. A different kind of instability is reflected in the 1662 Prayer Book, where at both Morning and Evening Prayer, and at Holy Communion, the Lord's Prayer appears twice, once with the doxology, and once without it.

This uncertainty and instability about how the Lord's Prayer ends is really about two things. One is that it ends abruptly in the two Gospels where it is found, because Jesus moves straight on to teaching. Secondly, no devout Jew at the time would have thought of ending any prayer without some kind of doxology, which is why as early as the *Didache*, and therefore within the lifetime of the later parts of the New Testament, the Lord's Prayer concludes with a doxology, although it is only about 'power and glory', and not 'kingdom' (*Didache* 8:2). This marks a decisive step towards rounding off the prayer in a suitable manner for liturgical use, rather than quoting it direct from scripture; perhaps it was influenced by doxologies in the New Testament Epistles, including one which mentions kingdom, power and glory (I Pet. 4:11, though the word for power is 'kratos' and not 'dunamis').

But what of commentators? John Chrysostom's exposition is the very first to include the doxology, and it was delivered probably in 390, during his time as a presbyter in Antioch, before his move to Constantinople as bishop.[2] He was influential in establishing the liturgy at Constantinople, hence the fact that the usual form of Eucharist celebrated to this day throughout the Byzantine rite is attributed to him. And, as we have seen, it includes the Lord's Prayer, ending with a doxology, and without any interjection by the celebrant.

The differing practices as to how the Lord's Prayer should conclude have tended to be resolved by the almost universal use of this doxology in modern versions, except, that is, when musical settings preclude it. It is a good ending, because it has a rhythm. As a prayer prayed and given by Christ in the Gospels, it would be incongruous to conclude with the words 'through Jesus Christ our Lord'. John Calvin insisted that the doxology should be part of the prayer.[3] Commentators in the Reformed, Lutheran and Anglican traditions ever since have tended to assume its use in their writings and in their preaching. All in all, it has been a confusing picture, but the doxology has won as if by stealth!

\*    \*    \*

But what do we mean by the kingdom, the power and the glory being God's and God's alone? Each word is about an attribute of God, and each points to a particular aspect of Christ's work in us. The *kingdom* is what we pray will be our inheritance (Eph. 5:5), that authority of God for whose coming we pray near the start of the prayer, and to which we now *submit* ourselves, as we contemplate the *teaching* of Christ, teaching which inaugurates that kingdom among us. The *power* of God, for salvation itself (Rom. 1:16), takes us back to the doing of his will, for which we prayed earlier; not a force that deprives us of our individuality or identity but one which motivates, and we can only be motivated by people whom we *trust*. This trust puts us in mind of the *actions* of Christ, his relatedness to us. The *glory* is what we can see in the face of Jesus Christ (2 Cor. 4:6), the glory that descends to the depths of human experience in order to raise it high (Phil. 2:5–11), a glory that takes seriously all that we are. This is a glory which we can *reverence* without taking it for granted or trying to pick it apart, because this glory points us to the *cross*, that sign of contradiction, that strange symbol of God's refusal to let us down, even when we fail him.

One of the functions of the doxology is to serve as a bridge between what we read of the Lord's Prayer in the New Testament and what we say now as people of today. At the end of his study of the Lord's Prayer, Christopher Evans remarks: 'Christianity is in two parts, and the relation between them is subtle. The continuity between them is provided by the continuance of Jesus himself, who is the subject of both parts, first as rabbi, teacher, and prophet, and then as Messiah, Lord, and Head of his body. The Lord's Prayer bears the marks of the time of its first delivery, when the issues of Jesus' life, and therefore of human life, had not yet come to a head. Perhaps not long afterwards they came to a head in the crucial events of which Holy Week and Easter are the memorial, and from that time onwards disciples were no longer able to pray the Lord's Prayer as they first prayed it, but only in and through the Lord. Only in this way have Christians ever been able to pray it since. What works the sea change is that Jesus moves into the centre, and all things of God are apprehended through him.'[4]

\*    \*    \*

The doxology is an essential part of the prayer, because it rounds it off elegantly and provides an ending which refers back to some of the aspirations of the prayer itself. But it means much more than that. If we are to take as seriously as we should the act of ascribing that kingdom, power and glory to God alone, we are doing two things.

First, we are offering that prayer anew to the throne of grace in heaven, and becoming part of that multitude which no one can number, who have prayed it in times past, as well as those who will be praying it in the centuries to come. We forget about heaven and underplay the communion of saints at our peril, especially in an age that can be self-preoccupied, and increasingly cut off – sometimes deliberately so – from our own past. Heaven is indeed where past, present and future are seen whole by God, and whilst we are unable to see ourselves whole, we know that however broken and fragmented our world is, we are none the less meant for unity, reconciliation, and the summing up of all things in Christ (Rom. 13:9; Eph. 1:10). And that places human notions of kingdom, power and glory necessarily under a different spotlight, that of the cross. The Lord's Prayer judges the world in its quietly eloquent manner and its doxology comes to underline that judgement. For the coronation is made of thorns, the power is made of meekness, and the glory is made of those glorious wounds.

Secondly, and through that judging, the doxology also drives us into the world, where praise is equally costly. It is not about what Stephen Sykes has referred to as 'the cheaply purchased satisfaction of the comfortable'.[5] Every year, I preside at the Easter Vigil in Portsmouth Cathedral. The Easter Vigil is a liturgy that I have attended ever since I was a student, and over the years I have managed to shed some of the historical excitement of helping to reintroduce and adapt one of the Church's most ancient liturgies in North European soil in our own time. That has given way to a lasting enthusiasm for the moment when the Old Testament readings are over and the *Gloria in Excelsis* is about to be sung. People bring their bells and trumpets and balloons and much else, and the organ blasts out a fanfare, as the people of God rejoice in the gift of the risen Christ to the whole world, after the rigours of Lent and Holy Week, as well as a North European spring. But it is the faces of those to be baptized and confirmed that nearly always catch my attention. They come with stories of different kinds about their conversion or their gradual re-absorption into the Church, which makes me rejoice in the health and realness of the coming Church. They are able to engage in the symbolism of the liturgy in a natural way that would have been unthinkable when I was confirmed. They are instinctively able to be relaxed and serious and focused – at the same time. Their sacramental rebirth clearly means a great deal to them, which comes soon after the singing of the *Gloria in Excelsis*, the great combined 'Alleluia' and 'Amen' of Easter.

In 1634, Henry King (1592–1669), then Archdeacon of Colchester and later Bishop of Chichester, published a course of eleven sermons on the Lord's Prayer. Right at the end, he prevents us from forgetting the importance of that final word 'Amen':

Let us therefore address ourselves to Him, not only in our prayers but for the success of those prayers, beseeching Him who at first pronounced a *fiat* ('let it be') over the work of his creation to repeat that *fiat* over us, in accomplishing the work of our redemption. Lord, only say the word, and thy servants shall live. By the power of thy Word thou didst set up a light in darkness. Thou saidst, let there be light, and it was made. Gracious God, for thy mercy's sake, exercise that act of power upon us. When we shall be benighted in our graves and shut up within the region of darkness, O thou that art the true light, suffer us not forever to sleep in death, but grant that in thy kingdom, and in thy presence, we may have the fruition of a new light. That we may see light in thy light, and enjoy that light by enjoying thee who art that light. That from thy militant Church, we may be translated into thy triumphant; that of Christians here, we may be made saints there; and finally exchange the state of grace for a crown of glory in thy kingdom, which shall know no end. Amen.[6]

# PART THREE

# Interpreters

# Evelyn Underhill: Retreat Addresses
# (1936)

Evelyn Underhill was born in 1875, the daughter of a London barrister.[1] She was brought up conventionally 'C of E', and in 1893 became a student at the newly opened Ladies Department of King's College, London. Thirteen years later she became engaged to another barrister, Hubert Stuart Moore, and was at that time intending to become Roman Catholic, a move that Hubert opposed strongly. The following year saw the beginning of the Anti-Modernist policy of Pope Pius X which shook her free of any desire to embrace a particular religious affiliation for some time. Instead, she became more and more interested in the mystical side of religion, and how it should be accessible to everyone rather than to an exclusive group; and while Christianity figured strongly in this area, so did other religions as well.

Her first major book, entitled *Mysticism*, was published in 1911. It explores the richness of religious experience in the Christian and other traditions and contains a lengthy appendix with biographies of spiritual writers down the ages. The book was ahead of its time. The ensuing years saw her writing introductions to the publication of medieval devotional classics such as *The Cloud of Unknowing* (1912) and Richard Rolle's *The Fire of Love and The Mending of Life* (1914), both of them landmarks in fourteenth-century English spirituality of whom few people at the time had heard. During the First World War, Underhill worked in Naval Intelligence, and was profoundly affected by the suffering of those who came back from the trenches; she was a strong personality who thought deeply and wrote passionately. A decisive moment occurred in 1921 when she publicly embraced the Church of England and returned to the Church in which she had been baptized and confirmed. She was made a Fellow of King's College, London, in 1927, and carried on writing about medieval mystics. Although now increasingly recognized as an influential Anglican laywoman (George Bell as Dean of Canterbury invited her to give a retreat for women in Canterbury Cathedral), she never entirely shrugged off those years of exploration as a seeking agnostic, nor did she cease to be a truly ecumenical explorer; her spiritual director was the Roman Catholic lay author, Baron Friedrich von Hügel.

In 1936, her second major book, entitled *Worship,* appeared. It was just as remarkable for its time as *Mysticism* was in 1911. In it she looks at Christian worship from a wide historical perspective, bringing psychological and social insights to the exercise that were unusual then and demonstrating too her new-found enthusiasm for Eastern Orthodoxy. Constantly in demand as a retreat conductor and writer, and at the same time increasingly suffering from asthma and bronchitis, she died of a haemorrhage in June 1941.

\*   \*   \*

As often happens with unusual thinkers, Underhill's writings received a degree of adulation that provoked in its turn something of a counter-reaction after her death. Her language could be quaint and more cosy than the direct and plain style that was coming into vogue as the twentieth century drew on. But a more balanced view has begun to prevail, revealing her real strengths as a prophetic figure, a woman theologian in a Church still dominated by male clergy, a believer who lived with many of the questions of the unbeliever. Above all, she was a scholar in her own right who was ready to unlock the riches of the past and make them accessible to an age which was sceptical of any view of tradition that assumed its position rather than argued for it on its own terms.

Many of these strands converge in *Abba*,[2] a collection of retreat addresses delivered in 1936 and published in 1940. After an introductory chapter, she goes through the Lord's Prayer with pungent chapter-headings that sum up the meaning of each petition in a brief but evocative manner: The Father, The Name, The Kingdom, The Will; Food, Forgiveness, Prevenience and Glory. The reader is thus made immediately aware that the first four petitions are about attributes of God that have a direct bearing on us, whereas the second four are about his gifts to us that we ask for, share with others, and render back to him. Their pithiness, too, reveals an author who was critical of superficiality in religion and religious discourse, as well as of those who (advertently or inadvertently) rob Christianity of its moral and ethical dimension. She never forgot those years away from the Church and the sight of the war-wounded. A Christianity turned in on itself was for her a denial of the gospel.

Near the start of her introductory chapter she lays her cards on the table: 'There is a conception of prayer which we easily forget; for the cheap fussiness of the anthropocentric (i.e. human-centred) life has even invaded our religion. There too, we prefer to live upon the surface and ignore the deep' (p.2). Although her remarks here could be applied to all prayer, they apply particularly to the Lord's Prayer. A tame Christianity that is increasingly focused on the self, its needs and feelings, rather than on the mystery of God and the pain of humanity, will always remain on the surface and will ignore the depths that God in Christ has plumbed and where so much of the real action and experience of the human race is located.

Her chapter entitled 'The Father' keeps drawing us as children of the same heavenly Father, as adopted children with responsibilities, to the life of faith. 'The crowds who followed Christ hoping for healing or counsel did not ask Him to teach them how to pray; nor did He give this prayer to them. It is not for those who want religion to be helpful, who seek after signs; those who expect it to solve their political problems and cure their diseases, but are not prepared to share its cost. He gave it to those whom He was going to incorporate into His rescuing system, use in His ministry; the sons of the Kingdom, self-given to the creative purposes of God' (p.10). In both Matthew and Luke there is a similar emphasis on the cost of following Christ. Matthew locates the Lord's Prayer halfway through the Sermon on the Mount, the call to the whole human race to the kingdom of God, to the values of a world turned upside down, whereas in Luke's Gospel, it is the disciples, and not the crowd, who come forward and ask, 'Lord, teach us to pray.' Christianity is not about being helpful or solving social problems or about health cures. The fatherhood of God is about much more, epitomized in that strange expression 'his rescuing system', which suggests an understanding of the Church that is mobile and messy, rather than institutionalized and packaged.

Underhill then looks at human need. 'Only in so far as he [one] is gathered into this relationship of worship, confidence and love, does he realise and express his shortcomings and his guilt' (p.11). Human beings are more ready to handle their shortcomings and guilt when they are faced with a vision of a God whom they can worship with confidence and love, supremely embodied in the fatherhood of God. Looking forward to the second part of the prayer, she writes, 'Men have three wants, which only God can satisfy. They need food, for they are weak and dependent. They need forgiveness, for they are sinful. They need guidance, for they are puzzled. Give-Forgive-Lead-Deliver' (p.12). All the time she is aware of the shape of the prayer, and the relationship between the first and the second parts. It is interesting that she describes people as 'puzzled' and in need of 'guidance'. Her later treatment of this need is full of the dangers of this world; perhaps her work as a spiritual director is coming through, just as her recognition of the need for food may well have evoked memories of hungry soldiers coming back from north France, and the need for forgiveness in her own deeply felt personal anguish at human folly.

\*    \*    \*

What of this fatherhood? 'Abba, Father. The personalist note, never absent from a fully operative religion, is struck at the start; and all else that is declared or asked is brought within the aura of this relationship' (p.13). Here we have what is probably the strongest hint of Underhill's own pilgrimage back to Christianity, since for her faith in God that is real has to be about human beings, and has to be embodied in our experience, at the same time elevating it and redeeming it. 'Fully operative religion' is to be contrasted with one that is spiritually dead, and which insists on living on the surface of life rather than plumbing its depths. If God really is our Father, a Father even more Father-like than our natural Father, then we can turn to him with anything. 'In these first words, the praying soul accepts once for all its true status as a member of the whole family of man. Our Father. It can never again enter into prayer as a ring-fenced individual, intent on a private relation with God; for this is a violation of the law of Charity' (p.14).

Underhill now exploits to the full that vital word 'our', sharply pointing to the dangers of individualism in religion, and daring to suggest that this prayer is not the private possession of the Church, but rather one in which the whole human race can, potentially, share. The Father is love. He belongs to all of us. And therefore that love must continue to move us outwards, into new horizons, new experiences, new relationships. Something of that movement is evoked by Jesus' command that we should ask and seek and knock (Matt. 7:7) – a favourite patristic text for teaching about the Christian life and prayer – when Evelyn writes as follows: 'This secret life is to be prosecuted with courage, confidence and zest: asking, seeking, and knocking with the assurance of the child, not with the desperation of the lost and starving slave' (p.15). We must ask with courage, seek with confidence, and knock with zest, as this movement in the life of faith takes us beyond what is familiar and safe, into the unfamiliar and even dangerous.

We are assured children, not lost slaves without food. Echoing the fourteenth-century mystic, Jan Ruysbroeck (1293–1381), for the English translation of whose work, *The Adornment of the Spiritual Marriage* she wrote an introduction in 1916, she maintains that 'the ultimate mystery is favourable to us; and our truest relation is that of filial trust' (p.16). In other words, God is source and final purpose, and while on this earth there may be events and experiences that make this trust less than easy, because the victory of the fatherhood of God is promised, we are able to walk that life of faith.

The fatherhood of God is mediated to us exclusively in the work of Christ. Echoing *The Spiritual Canticle* of John of the Cross (1542–91), the Spanish mystic and friend of Teresa of Avila, she writes: 'We recognize Him . . . because we already carry in our hearts a rough sketch of the beloved countenance. Looking into those deeps, as into a quiet pool in the dark forest, we there find looking back at us the Face we implicitly long for and already know' (p.17). Once more she uses a strange expression 'rough sketch' and she does so in order to express our likeness to and distance from the God we know in Jesus Christ. To use a pool as a mirror usually means seeing a shimmering and moving picture, not an exact and still likeness, a moving face that keeps gazing at us as we look at it. Something of the same sense of movement Underhill describes right at the end of the last chapter ('Glory') when she writes: 'Behind every closed door which seems to shut experience from us, He is standing; and within every experience which reaches us, however disconcerting, His unchanging presence is concealed' (p.86).

Underhill's terse style conceals an awareness of many of the problems people have with faith, and their struggle to make sense of their lives; and the fact that these addresses were published in wartime England is of some significance. Having been through one war earlier in her life, she was to live through the tragic opening of another. But there is no self-indulgent introspection here. With her width of reading that includes other figures such as William Blake, S. T. Coleridge, Teresa of Avila, and Søren Kierkegaard, she keeps showing how we can embrace the heavenly fatherhood of God, by the dignity that it confers on us, as well as the responsibility to which we are called in discipleship.

# F. D. Maurice: Sermons (1848)

In the spring of 1848, F. D. Maurice preached a course of nine sermons on the Lord's Prayer in the Chapel of Lincoln's Inn, London. Lincoln's Inn is one of the 'Inns of Court', where he had served as Chaplain since 1846. The sermons were delivered at Evening Prayer, in those days held in the afternoon, and the congregation gathered in the impressive seventeenth-century chapel would have been made up of members of the legal fraternity, together with others who came deliberately to hear Maurice preach, since he was by that time a well-known figure.

Maurice was born in 1805 near Lowestoft, the son of a Unitarian Minister.[1] His mother and his two siblings all became Evangelical Anglicans, but Maurice himself is more difficult to label. While at Trinity College, Cambridge, he came under the influence of Frederick Field, who was a considerable biblical and patristic scholar. Maurice left, because he was unable to subscribe to the Thirty-Nine Articles of Religion, and became increasingly interested in social reform. In 1830 he went to Exeter College, Oxford, after finally subscribing to the Articles, and was ordained in 1834 to a curacy in Warwickshire. In 1836 he was appointed Chaplain at Guy's Hospital in London, and began to lecture on moral philosophy. He never forgot his Unitarian roots. In no way undermining his theological orthodoxy, they imbued him with a strong sense of the goodness of God and the power of reason to uncover truth. His first major work, *The Kingdom of Christ*, was published in twelve parts in 1837, and as a single book in the following year. It is a defence of the Book of Common Prayer as an expression of the theological and social character of the Church of England, and throughout its pages Maurice sets out to answer its various critics, including Unitarians and Quakers.

In 1840, Maurice was appointed Professor of English Literature and History at King's College, London, and six years later he went to Lincoln's Inn as Chaplain (deputy to the 'Preacher') at the same time being given a professorship of Theology. He was profoundly moved by the political events in Europe in 1848, which serve as a significant backdrop to the sermons on the Lord's Prayer. He made friends with J. M. F. Ludlow, which led to the formation of the Christian Socialists: 'The new Socialism must be Christianized,' Maurice maintained. With Charles Kingsley and others, he set up the Working Men's College in London's Russell Square.

When Maurice published his *Theological Essays* in 1853, he was dismissed from his professorship at King's College because of his doubts about the endless character of future punishment and his view that eternity was not the same as time. In 1860, he was given a more permanent pastoral post at the Chapel of St Peter's, Vere Street, and six years later he was appointed Knightsbridge Professor of Moral Philosophy at Cambridge. He died on Easter Day 1872, his last words being about Holy Communion for people of all nations, and that women would teach men its meaning.

In many respects, Maurice's most distinctive works are his sermons, of which he published several volumes. While the overall argument within them is usually clear, the individual arrangement of ideas within them sometimes leaves the impression of strong conviction readily expressed and illustrated colourfully, but not always a systematic development of an argument. In many respects, Maurice combines all three traditional 'strands' of Anglicanism, Catholic, Liberal, Evangelical. He loves the Prayer Book and Anglican tradition and from Advent in 1848 onwards was to preach a course of sermons on the services of the Prayer Book. He believes in articulating the faith afresh to a new generation. But he offsets his belief in the goodness of God with a strong emphasis on sacrifice, in the life and teaching of Christ as well as in the discipleship of the believer. He left a considerable mark on the nineteenth-century theological scene, both for his preaching, his work in Adult Education, and his contribution to the growing social aware-ness of the Church of England in a much changed world.

\* \* \*

The year 1848 is often described as 'the year of the European Revolutions'. On 12 January in Italy, Palermo revolted against the Bourbon King of Naples. On 23 February in France, the barricades went up in Paris and the National Guard joined in the demonstration, leading to the abdication of King Louis Philippe, who managed to escape across the English Channel to Newhaven. The telegraph wires brought all this news to London, as well as news of the equally alarming expulsion from Milan of the Austrian troops on 18 March. There was a Chartist demonstration on 10 April which caused Queen Victoria to leave London, and F. D. Maurice tried to enlist (unsuccessfully) as a special constable.

Maurice began his first sermon the Lord's Prayer[2] on 13 February by affirming that 'the Paternoster . . . may be com-mitted to memory quickly, but it is slowly learned by heart' (p.1). The second sermon expounds the hallowing of the Name. Delivered on Septuagesima Sunday it could well have been coloured by the day's Collect, Epistle and Gospel, which will have been read during the morning service. The Collect prays 'that we, who are justly punished for our offences, may be mercifully delivered by thy goodness for the glory of thy Name . . .'. The Epistle is Paul's call to run the race and bring the body into subjection (1 Cor. 9:24ff), and the Gospel is the parable of the vineyard (Matt. 20:1ff). Delivered after the revolt in Palermo and three days before the disturbances in Paris, this particular sermon has something of an atmosphere to it.

Maurice begins by noting the place of the petition to hallow God's Name in the shape of the prayer as a whole. 'The prin-ciple of prayer which asks first for bread or forgiveness must be wholly different from the principle of one which begins with "hallowed be thy Name"' (p.13). This point was made by Lancelot Andrewes in his sermons in 1611, but Maurice relates the shape of the prayer more explicitly to our needs. 'He (God) recognizes the desires of which I have spoken as reasonable and true, but he postpones them; and this, too, when he is warning us against babbling in prayer, against all vain, idle formulas; when he is directing us especially to ask for the things we have need of' (p.14). It is right that we should ask for bread and forgiveness, but we need first to recognize the fatherhood and holiness of God, and not let our prayers turn into formulas which are vain and idle. Interestingly, he uses the word 'babbling', following the sixteenth-century translations of Tyndale and Coverdale, in addition to the 'vain repetitions' of the Authorised Version of 1611, which was the only official version allowed at the time. This may reflect Maurice's conviction about the need for set prayers used with understanding and conviction.

Maurice claims a central and universal place for the hallowing of God's Name. 'If we are led by any process to feel that the news concerning a Father is really *the* good news, apart from which the promise of food or pardon would signify nothing, we shall feel that "hallowed be thy Name" is the first and most necessary and most blessed prayer for the whole human race' (p.15). He therefore wants his hearers to halt at this petition, and to see it both as a definition of the nature of God and a necessity for believers to focus their needs, and the needs of the whole world, as under the protection and beneficence of God and nothing else. He defines the hallowing of the Name by us in an echo of Luke's version of the *Shema* (the 'Summary of the Law') (Luke 10:27): 'He has within him a witness that there is a Being whom he ought to love with his heart and soul and strength' (p.16). But there is a social focus for the hallowing of the Name, which is not about individuals and their pilgrimage of faith as a separate department of human experience: 'upon our thoughts of God it will depend, in one time or another, whether we rise higher or sink lower as society and as individuals' (p.17). Here is a vision of a Church that has responsibilities for the whole nation, as a constituent part of the human race, rather than a religious group turned in on itself. Prayer and life are closely interconnected, since life is the answer that we ourselves make to the prayer we offer to God: 'What is the Name of Him to whom we pray? The meaning of prayer, of human existence, turns upon the answer which we make to this demand' (p.18) .

The hallowing of the Name, while it implies separation, does not mean that the community of believers live in a religious ghetto. 'Solitude is no security for the hallowing of God's Name' (p.19). 'To hallow God's Name, habitually to hallow it, amidst such countless variations of the external atmosphere, such colds and heats in ourselves – how is it possible? Must not we give up the attempt?' (p.20). We are not able to hallow God's Name on our own, nor should we. We therefore are called to hallow it collectively. Whilst Maurice insists on the corporate aspect of everything that is Christian, he admits at this point that we are not able to hallow it properly, since we can only do it by the grace of God.

This brings Maurice, characteristically, to place Christ centre stage, as the only means whereby we can begin to accomplish the hallowing in our lives. 'If He brought gifts to men, if He proclaimed forgiveness to men, this was His first gift, this was the ground of His forgiveness. He hallowed the Name of God. He showed forth the Father who dwelt in Him full of grace and truth . . . Here was goodness and truth in its primitive form, in its entire fullness' (p.21). Maurice is on the verge of exaggerating the importance of the hallowing of the Name by giving it a foundation place in the person of Christ as the Son of God! But the experiment comes off in the way that he links the hallowing of the Name with the manifestation of the Father who dwelt in Him, full of grace and truth.

All this applies directly to our own tendencies to tame Christianity, whether by romantic idealism or by reductionism: 'still less let us refuse to have our own loose and incoherent notions brought to trial, lest in losing them we should lose the eternal truths of God's Word' (p.22f). Maurice is only too well

aware of the inadequacy – and yet the necessity – of our own
fumbling expressions of the Christian faith, whether these
concern how we put it into words, or how we put it into
practice. Loose and incoherent they may well be, but our words
and actions are still the vehicles in which Christ's fullness
chooses to dwell. Maurice, wedded to Baptism as the sacramental entry upon the whole Christian life, with all its privileges and responsibilities, links the hallowing of the Name with
Baptism: 'Therefore let us pray this prayer, "Hallowed be thy
Name", believing that it has been answered, and being
confident that it will be answered . . . It is answered by our
baptism into the holy and blessed Name, the Father, the Son
and the Holy Ghost . . . It is answered by confirmation and
prayers, and holy communion, by individual trials, by visita-
tions to nations, by the gift of new life to Churches, by the
conversion of sinners by dying beds. It will be answered when
we all yield ourselves up indeed in truth to the Spirit of God,
that we like our Lord may glorify His Name upon the earth,
and may accomplish the work which He has given us to do'
(p.23).

*     *     *

A decade earlier Maurice, in *The Kingdom of Christ*, wrote
about how the Lord's Prayer engenders a collective, objective
understanding of the Christian community on its knees before
the heavenly Father. It is a prayer directly related to the out-
working of God's purposes in human history – 'a kingdom
which comes to subvert nothing, but to restore that which
is decayed and falling; to adopt into itself every fragment of
existing faith and feeling; to purify it and to exalt it; to cut off
from it only that which the conscience of the native confesses
to be inconsistent with it; to testify that wherever there is a
creature having human limbs and features, there is one of that
race for which Christ died, one whom he is not ashamed to call
a brother'.[3] Later in 1848, in his fourth sermon on the Prayer
Book, Maurice was to assert that 'Churches were not built as

signs of exclusion, but of reconciliation.'[4] Here is a vision of a community that believes and lives by the hallowing of the Name, sacramentally and socially, a community whose boundaries are not tightly drawn, but both demanding and at the same time open.

Maurice's preaching in these sermons is liturgical in the true sense of the word. He is not concerned with the finer details so much as with the meaning of the prayer and how that can be applied to his hearers. It is the same method that he adopts elsewhere. For him the Prayer Book provides the rhythm and the good Christian sense for the public worship of the Church of England. Within those services and in the private devotion of ordinary people, the Lord's Prayer stands out as the prayer which he describes 'may be committed to memory quickly, but it is slowly learned by heart' (p.1). Preaching on the following Sunday about the coming of the kingdom, only days after the events in Paris, he says that 'we have reached the petition of the Lord's Prayer at a time which would seem to give it special emphasis and significance' (p.25). He looks at the pain and the folly of the world not as a blip in the history of the human race but as the place where Christ's sacrifice is to be found, showing the very nature of God himself, for 'the Cross is at once the complete utterance of the Prayer and the answer to it' (p.46). Preaching on temptation he looks to the redemptive work of Christ: 'that which seemed to be poison becomes medicine; all circumstances are turned to good; honey is gathered out of the carcass; death itself is made the minister of life' (p.100). When he preaches on 'deliver us from evil', he sees the darkness of the world as real and at times horrific but always as a prelude to the coming kingdom: 'I will pray in the certainty that He is maintaining a conflict with the self-will which is the curse and dislocation of the world, and that every plague, pestilence, insurrection, revolution, is a step in the history of that conflict, ending towards the final victory' (p.114).

Maurice holds so much together in his preaching that at times it seems to pour relentlessly! Preaching on the Lord's Prayer in Advent that year, the same universal vision of the whole human race in worship, service and sacrifice is evoked: 'In this way we ask that we may offer an acceptable sacrifice, in this way that we may live pure and holy lives. We ask it by desiring that the Name of the Everlasting Father may be hallowed; that His Kingdom may come; that His will may be done. For we are certain that He does will our highest freedom and blessedness; that in his Kingdom, all from the prince to the beggar, have their vocations – their thrones and their priesthoods; we are certain that in His Name is the perfect Unity for all the creatures whom He has formed.'[5]

# Leonardo Boff: 'The Prayer of Integral Liberation' (1979)

Experience has taught us that it is not necessary to say 'Lord, Lord' in order to do good and to enter the kingdom. In our work in the factories and in the slums, we have found examples of persons who are totally disinterested and dedicated to others, and who do not say 'Lord, Lord'. These persons are prepared to sacrifice their jobs, their family, and even themselves for the good of all. The gospel is present in them, and the Spirit finds realization.

We have learned to judge these persons by what they are and do, and not by the institution to which they belong or by the doctrine they profess. We invite everyone to do the same, if they wish to understand what the prophet Amos meant when he denied the special election of Israel by Yahweh and taught the practice of justice as the only source of salvation.

It is thus that we understand our struggle and our faith. We believe that we are building up the kingdom. The 'we' includes those of the worker ministry and all those who struggle with us. We do not separate things from persons. We do not feel that we are better. We work with all on a basis of equality.

All those who struggle for the building of the kingdom will live in it. There will be no privileges. Righteousness is based on works; those who pass judgement on the basis of dogmas condemn themselves. There will be no room for those who reject their equals in the name of a doctrine or those who think they are saved by what they have inherited.[1]

This is how Leonardo Boff begins the chapter on 'Your Kingdom Come' in his book *The Lord's Prayer: The Prayer of Integral Liberation*, which was first published in Portuguese, in Petropolis, where he teaches Theology, in 1979. He adopts the same tactic throughout the book. Each chapter begins with a story or an extended anecdote giving some kind of reflection on the meaning of what he is about to explain and expound.

In this case it is a letter written by one of the 'base communities' in São Paulo. The basic communities are congregations of Christians with a tightly-knit community life in which they set out to live their Christian discipleship in the struggles of their locality. In Latin America, particularly in a large city like São Paulo, this means working among the desperately poor, those millions of people whose livelihood is part of an endless cycle of deprivation.

Leonard Boff was born in 1938 and is a Franciscan priest. He used to teach systematic theology at the Institute of Philosophy and Theology at Petropolis, thirteen miles north-west of Rio de Janeiro. Petropolis was a city named after Emperor Pedro I, a member of the Portuguese Royal Family who ruled Brazil for a short time after its independence from Portugal in the nineteenth century. Boff studied at Oxford, Louvain, Würzburg and Munich, and is one of the main exponents of Liberation Theology. Its distinctive characteristic is an emphasis on the power of the gospel to liberate from structural as well as personal sin. His book *St Francis: A Model for Human Liberation* (1982) was first published in Portuguese in the previous year and reveals the way in which Boff has modelled his entire Christianity on Francis of Assisi, the man of poverty who lived out the gospel not in abstracts but in severely practical ways. There is a profound boldness about Boff's acceptance of what he calls living joyfully with the unchangeable. 'We do not live in the world we would like to, but rather in the world that has been imposed on us. We do not do everything we desire, but only that which we can and are allowed to do. Only an idealistic vision of history and of the individual conceives of liberty as pure spontaneity and creativity. Liberty is realised within a defined space, and the widening of that sphere always means an onerous process of liberation. It is a sign of maturity to accept calmly and with interior detachment those realities, objectively, we cannot change.'[2]

That tough-minded and long view of faith has its roots in his own country's history. Brazil was 'discovered' in 1500 for the Portuguese Empire and its goldfields soon led to exploitation by the Portuguese rulers, with slaves from West Africa (slavery was abolished in 1850). It is the largest country in South America, overwhelmingly Roman Catholic, but Protestants have been better treated there in the past than in other Latin American countries. In 1889, a Republic was founded to replace the 'Empire' set up in 1822. As with other Latin American countries, a feature of the political scene in the past century has been right-wing governments, in a country with huge sprawls of extreme poverty in the shanty towns surrounding the large cities such as São Paulo.

But Liberation Theology arose from a more complex process still. Popular Catholicism has often concentrated on the suffering Christ. There is even a myth of a 'pre-colonial' Christianity in Latin America, with millenarian hopes of a coming kingdom. 'Catholic Action', a movement in the first part of the twentieth century to mobilize the well-to-do for the poor, had a strong influence through such Roman Catholic writers and activists as Paulo Freire. French Catholic biblical studies also had their own influence on the theological leadership in Brazil and elsewhere, emphasizing the reading of the scriptures in the native tongue and letting the scriptures address the people of God where they were. At the time of the Second Vatican Council, Rome backed the Latin American bishops, the Brazilian hierarchy included, in focusing the Church's work on the plight of the poor. Since then, relations have become more difficult and Boff has lost his official recognition as a Roman Catholic teacher, and has left the priesthood.

\* \* \*

Thus Boff, the Brazilian Franciscan, European trained, theologically Vatican II, and thoroughly earthed in the realities of Christian discipleship in these 'base' communities, comes to expound the Lord's Prayer. He begins by stating that 'there are good reasons why the essence of Jesus' message – The Lord's Prayer – was not formulated as a doctrinal statement but as a prayer' (p.6). The Lord's Prayer does indeed contain the essence of Jesus' teaching, but it takes the form of a prayer, because the teaching of Jesus is about a kingdom that is always on its way, not a political plan or a religious system. Throughout the book Boff holds together the 'contemplative' and the 'active' by statements such as this: 'Faith has two eyes, one that looks up to God and contemplates his light; and another that is turned towards the earth and discerns the tragedy of darkness' (p.20). God is therefore defined as 'a Father even in the darkness of internal light or the grief over nameless sufferings' (p.36). (Is there a hint, here, of another Franciscan, John of the Cross, in his 'dark night of the soul'?) The Christian faith has nothing to do with the 'feel-good factor' that Boff will sense from parts of North America and Europe. 'As long as we remain locked into a conception of God who helps and of religion as something good for human balance, we cannot break out of that vicious circle of our own egotism and meet with God' (p.48).

Such observations as these set the scene for his treatment of the petition for the coming of the kingdom. 'With the supplication "thy kingdom come" we get into the very heart of the Lord's Prayer. At the same time, we are confronted with the ultimate intention of Jesus, because the proclamation of the kingdom of God constitutes the core of his message and the primary motive of his activities. In order to fully comprehend the meaning of this supplication – which burrows into the most profound depths of our anxiety and our hopes – we must begin at a distance and dig deeply. Only then will its radicality and novelty be appreciated' (p.54). This is not the first time that Boff points to human anxiety, and it is interesting that, like Maurice, another socially focused expositor, he should warn against superficiality, particularly in a prayer that is so familiar. Aware, too, of the contemporary tendency to narrow the gap between the human being and the animal world, Boff points out that 'what distinguishes human beings from animals is not so much intelligence as imagination' (p.54). Imagining the kingdom is a central part of the grammar of Christianity. When things go badly wrong in society, and the kingdom seems farthest away, we have all the more opportunity (and not less) to see the hand of God at work: 'these hopes become more fervent in direct proportion to the cruelty of this world's contradictions' (p.55). At the beginning of the chapter, Boff insists through the base-community letter that Christianity is to be lived rather than talked about; now he provides a firm view, akin to the Old Testament prophets, that 'the living God, more than being a God of worship, is an ethical God who despises iniquity and rejoices with the just' (p.56).

There is a boldness about Boff's proclamation of the coming of the kingdom, and it is no surprise that he draws inspiration from the boldness of the proclamation of Jesus at the start of Mark's Gospel: 'It is against this background of hope and anxiety that we hear the voice of Jesus of Nazareth: "The time has come; the kingdom of God is upon you; repent, and believe this good news"' (p.57). Yet this kingdom is not always obvious: 'the kingdom is something understood to a certain extent and yet at the same time hidden and desirable' (p.58). This means that 'conflict is inevitable; a crisis cannot be avoided. We are urged to make a decision' (p.59). Here is the mark of European theology, going back to Kierkegaard, of being confronted by the existential reality of God, to whom we cannot remain passive. When we pray for the coming of the kingdom, we have to realise that it is both 'now' and 'not yet', which is the message of the New Testament. 'The kingdom is a joyful state, celebrated in the present, but at the same time it is a promise that is to be realised in the future' (p.60). He brings the central work of Christ into the very heart of this praying for the kingdom by evoking once more the atmosphere of Mark's Gospel: 'Even rejection, the cross and sin are not insuperable obstacles to God' (p.60).

\* \* \*

We are always left with a choice, not to try to change the world in three minutes, but to take the long view, which is the fundamental truth of the Bible itself and of the teaching of Jesus. Boff chooses to reject the popular Marxist fatalistic view of history: 'history is not directed by fate, by a single type of behaviour or a single type of development. It was Marx in his old age (1881) who recognized that one cannot make a theory concerning the laws of history, a theory of necessities, without first having a theory of the possibles that constitute the fields of practical possibilities for a given era of history – fields that do not admit of a single meaning but have a range of meanings and realisations. Thus there is always a diversity of alternatives' (p.61). For Christ plumbs the depths of Christian suffering, and in that suffering Boff finds the person of Christ himself, the suffering figure of popular piety, that is seen now walking about – and judging – the streets of the shanty towns, rather than remaining as a statue in a side chapel. 'The supplication "thy kingdom come" is a cry that springs from the most radical hope, a hope that we often see contradicted, but which we never give up despite everything, as we hope for the revelation of an absolute meaning that is to be realised by God in all of creation' (p.62). 'Despite everything' is a key expression, and they are the last two words of the book: 'Being able to say Amen implies being able to trust and be confident and certain that everything is in the hands of the Father; he has already conquered mistrust and fear, despite everything' (p.122). Here is a profound Christian thinker who is unable to give up on the Christian faith, a faith which provides for him the only acceptable interpretation of his experience of life.

Boff's message is not for a vague liberation on its own, definable by whatever slant we take. It is liberation that is *integral*, as the subtitle of the book – *The Prayer of Integral Liberation* – shows. This is a theme to which he returns in *Trinity and Society*, which appeared in 1988 in English translation after its publication in Portuguese in 1986. He describes the work of the Son as 'mediator of integral liberation' and the work of the Holy Spirit as 'driving force of integral liberation'.[3]

The word 'integral' probably has stronger resonances in Portuguese than in English. The freedom for which we pray, and which Christ not only preached but inaugurated, is a freedom from *all* that prevents us fulfilling our lives according to the pattern of God as revealed in Christ, whether it is in praying to the Father, hallowing the Name, doing the will, sharing food, being forgiven and forgiving, and surviving the ills of this world – and, as here, praying for the coming of that kingdom, precisely because we are gripped by its truthfulness and its integrity. 'The kingdom and everything that comes from God is structured as a proposal, not as an imposition; it is a gesture of invitation and not a pre-emptive command' (p.67). 'This anxiety and this suffering cannot be healed by any medicine or therapy' (p.103). The Christian gospel has to be lived out, not just talked about; 'evil has never been experienced in a vague, abstract form, nor have grace and goodness' (p.112).

Boff's exposition of the Lord's Prayer is a worthy and innovative part of the long Franciscan tradition of the use of this prayer. He speaks from his own context, but as part of that tradition, as he places every syllable within the landscape of suffering and poverty, and the greed and folly that produced it, as if that landscape were the very ground on which Christ treads today, 'despite everything'.

# Cyprian of Carthage: Baptismal Preparation (252)

The city of Carthage, or Kart-hadasht, as it is known in Arabic, had a long, distinguished and sometimes violent history in antiquity. From the time of its founding by Phoenicians from Tyre in 814 BCE through the Punic Wars with Rome (Hannibal crossed the Alps with his elephants to defeat Rome in 218), the destruction of the city in 146 BCE, its subsequent re-founding as a Roman colony, its time as the seat of a Christian bishopric and its eventual capture during the Muslim invasions in 697, its story was a colourful one. Fifteen hundred years is not a bad score for a proud city, which retained to the end a mixture of Phoenician (Punic) origins, intermarrying with the local Berber population, to say nothing of the mixture of other races and peoples, Roman included. Lying as it does on the north-east prong of Tunisia opposite the south-western end of Sicily inevitably gave it a strong position. Trade in its own manufacture of carpets, rugs, purple dyes, jewellery, pottery, lamps, tapestry, timber and hides made Carthage wealthy and influential.

The Phoenician colonists who founded Carthage brought with them the worship of their own gods, Baal-Hammon, Taanit-pene-Baal and Melkart. Human sacrifice was not unknown, and it was the survival of this religion, as well as the strength of the new religion, Christianity, that imperial Rome found unacceptable. When Bishop Cyprian wrote his 'Treatise on the Lord's Prayer' in 252, he was already a well established public figure.[1] Born of wealthy parents early in the third century, he converted to Christianity, and was baptized in 246. He took Christ's demand to give to the poor literally and was generous with his wealth. Ordained a presbyter by the ageing bishop in 247, he was chosen to be his successor the following year, in spite of a small group of hostile clergy who were suspicious of this newly-fledged Christian.

The Emperor Decius soon decreed that the old Roman virtues and religion should be restored throughout the Empire, which would mean – if applied universally and systematically – the destruction of Christianity. Cyprian responded not by confronting the imperial authorities but by retiring from Carthage, in order to rule his Church from a safer place. The persecution died down, and Cyprian was able to return to Carthage in November 251. The following years saw various Councils of the Church held at Carthage to deal with a number of matters, including how those who had lapsed from Christianity under the persecution should be treated. In this Cyprian took a controversial stance: the lapsed should be allowed to return, not excluded for ever. A serious plague hit Carthage in 252 and Cyprian urged the Christian community to respond with dedication and generosity. Five years later, in 257, the Emperor Valerian again proscribed Christianity. He was determined to confront local officials of the Church, particularly those in prominent places such as Cyprian himself. On 14 September 258, Cyprian was executed. He was immediately venerated as a martyr.

Trained in oratory – a respected profession in antiquity, which involved law, logic and philosophy – Cyprian brought to Christianity not only a forceful personality but a well tuned mind. He had a particular devotion to another famous north African theologian, Tertullian (c.160–225),[2] from whose literary output Cyprian is said to have read every day. Among these is a short 'Treatise on Prayer', which is supposed to have been written between 202 and 206, and therefore regarded as 'safe', because it was before Tertullian left the Catholic Church to join a group called the Montanists, who had what nowadays might be described as very extreme charismatic leanings.

Tertullian's treatment of prayer in general and the Lord's Prayer in particular influenced Cyprian greatly, to the point that there are parallels and echoes in certain places. But Cyprian was his own man, and his work on the Lord's Prayer is more instructive, and more obviously aimed at those learning the Lord's Prayer in the context of Christian Baptism. There are thirty-six chapters in all, of which chapters seven to twenty-seven are specifically about the Lord's Prayer.[3]

\*     \*     \*

He begins chapter one by emphasizing that to recite the prayer is to follow in every sense the commands and example of Jesus: 'The gospel precepts, dearly beloved brethren, are nothing else than divine commands, foundations on which hope is to be built up, buttresses by which faith is to be strengthened, nourishment wherefrom the heart is to be comforted, helms whereby to steer our way, ramparts whereby salvation is to be preserved; and thus, while they instruct the teachable minds of believers on earth, they also lead them on to the heavenly kingdom' (p.25).

The Lord's Prayer is clearly between the lines of this opening paragraph, even though Cyprian is setting it in the context of the whole of the gospel. Commands, foundations, buttresses, nourishment, helms and ramparts are all powerful metaphors. Commands are spoken, foundations are built, buttresses are set up, nourishment is consumed, helms are for steering and ramparts are built for protection. The Lord's Prayer is about all that; the prayer for daily bread is for nourishment, and the prayer not to be led into temptation is about a spiritual rampart. Merging the walk on earth with the journey to heaven echoes the twofold direction of the prayer as prayed by us, particularly in the will being done on earth as it is in heaven. We can discern these petitions between the lines of this concise and powerful opening.

What we are taught to pray is there by Christ's authority because it constitutes the best pattern for us. 'He who made us to live taught us also to pray, moved by that same loving-kindness wherewith He has deigned also to grant and confer all things else; so that when we speak in the presence of the Father, with the petition and prayer which His Son taught, we shall be heard the more readily' (p.26). It is both private and public, where prayer needs to have a structure and a comprehensibility: 'when we come together into one place with the brethren and celebrate divine sacrifices with God's priest, we ought to be mindful of reverence and order, not tossing our prayers into the air on all sides with ill-assorted words, nor flinging out a petition which ought to be modestly commended to God, with tumultuous loquacity, because God is the hearer not of the voice but of the heart' (p.29). These words read as if they had been written yesterday, for they apply just as much to today's Church, the warning against babbling (Matt. 6:7) included. Prayer must come from the heart, and we must try to mean it.

When he begins on the text of the Lord's Prayer, in chapter seven, we come across two instances where his version differs from what we are familiar with. First, 'your will be done in heaven and on earth'. Secondly, 'do not suffer us to be led into temptation' (not 'lead us not'). These are both taken from Tertullian's treatise, and were familiar in North Africa. Cyprian's view, not unrelated to the reality of persecution and suffering by Christians places temptation in the context of divine permission, rather than the ordinary experiences of being tested that life brings. Such variants as these are evidence of a text that was not once and for all established, but was subject to minor development and interpretation. They show that in developing and translating, notions of how God both walks before us and gives us freedom have to be grappled with.

Cyprian then insists that 'we do not say, *My Father Who art in heaven*, nor *Give me this day my bread*, nor does each one ask that his own debt only be remitted, nor does he request for himself alone that he may not be led into temptation and may be delivered from the evil one. Prayer with us is public and common; and when we pray we do not pray for one but for the

whole people, because we the whole people are one' (pp.32–3).
This point has been made repeatedly ever since, and it is at the
heart of the prayer, which Cyprian goes on to describe as 'this
compendium of heavenly teaching' (p.34), echoing Tertullian's
definition as 'a summary of the whole gospel'.

Those who recite the Lord's Prayer witness to their Baptism:
'Let him witness too among the very first words of his (new)
birth that he has renounced his earthly and fleshly father, and
that he recognizes and has begun to have as his Father only Him
Who is in heaven' (p.35). Cyprian here alludes to the baptismal
renunciation of evil and profession of faith, and indicates, too,
that the Lord's Prayer was only recited by the baptized in
church. Baptism confers divine sonship: 'Our Father; the
Father, that is, of those who believe, of those who, sanctified by
Him and renewed by the birth of spiritual grace, have begun to
be sons of God' (p.36). The baptismal profession must involve,
too, baptismal discipleship: 'We ought then, dearly beloved
brethren, to remember and to realize that when we call God
Father, we ought to act as sons of God' (p.37). Baptism carries
on in his treatment of the hallowing of the Name, where he
suggests (as does Augustine after him) that to pray the Lord's
Prayer daily is a way of renewing that sacramental rebirth. 'We
ask that God's kingdom may be made present to us in the same
way that we entreat that His Name may be hallowed in us'
(p.40).

\*      \*      \*

All this leads to Cyprian's treatment of the petition for the
doing of the will – 'in heaven and on earth', in his version. 'But
since we are opposed by the devil, and our own mind and
actions hindered in every way from being in submission to God,
we ask and beseech that God's will may be done in us' (p.42).
Like Tertullian before him, he prays that God's will may indeed
be done in us, in word as well as deed. 'Now the will of God is
that which Christ did and taught' (p.43). Such is the baptismal
life; 'this it is to endeavour to be co-heir with Christ, this it is to

do the will of God, this it is to fulfil the will of the Father' (p.43).

But what of the relationship between the earthly and the heavenly? 'Since we possess a body from earth and a spirit from heaven, we are ourselves earth and heaven; and in both – that is, in body and in spirit – we pray that God's will may be done' (p.44). The point of Cyprian's emphasis is twofold. God's will is done in heaven, and our calling is to try by divine grace to let the heavenly direct the earthly. That has a multi-layered reference to the way we try to order our own lives, but it also applies to the mission of the Church: 'we pray also for those who are still earth and who have not begun to be heavenly, that concerning them also the will of God may be done which Christ fulfilled by saving and renewing human nature' (p.45).

For Cyprian the doing of the will is about being submissive to God, to be imbued with what Christ did and taught, and thereby to live a life worthy of being a fellow-heir with Christ. That means praying this prayer daily, and daily receiving the Eucharist (p.47), asking for sustenance without taking thought for tomorrow (Luke 12:22), and unimpeded by worldly posses-sions, since God will always provide. Here is the man of wealth who is generous in giving to the poor and needy. Forgiveness is seen as a sacrifice before God when it is mutual, and it must be meant from the heart and be costly. When we are tempted, God's sovereign will is safeguarded by Cyprian's view that he – only temporarily – gives the adversary permission to take control of a part of the created order.

In the concluding chapters, Cyprian deals with daily prayer, and gives us evidence of the dialogue, 'lift up your hearts' at the Eucharist, and the custom of the congregation standing for liturgical prayer. He also interprets Morning Prayer as a cele-bration of the resurrection and Evening Prayer as a looking to the Advent of Christ. He begins his final chapter with the telling words: 'Let us then, who are ever in Christ – that is, in the Light – cease not from prayer even by night' (p.69).

Cyprian's treatise reflects his own pastoral concerns: unity, practical discipleship, sacrifice and martyrdom, and the privilege of being children of God at a time of suffering, when the call to be generous to the needy is all the more powerful. His references to the Eucharist as 'divine sacrifices' and to mutual forgiveness as 'the greater sacrifice before God' reflect his view of the sacrificial character of Christian living.[4] Just as Tertullian influenced Cyprian, Cyprian's 'Treatise on the Lord's Prayer', with its practical and baptismal focus, so influenced Augustine at the end of the following century that he alludes to it more than once; and Hilary of Poitiers (c.315–367/8) was so taken with it that he used it himself, instead of writing his own exposition. That is testimony to the enduring quality of the teaching of this, the most famous early Christian martyr from the continent of Africa.

# Teresa of Avila: Religious Community Life (1565)

On 4 October 1582, a Spanish nun died (probably from cancer) at a convent in Alba de Tormes on her way back from Burgos to the mother-house in her native Avila.[1] Teresa of Avila, as she has been called, had had a remarkable life, in which her influence on the Church in the newly reconstituted kingdom of Spain was considerable. The daughter of a well-to-do member of the minor nobility, she was born in March 1515. There was Jewish blood in the family, whose noble status had been bought by wealth, not inherited by a long-standing artistocratic lineage. Teresa's growing religious faith never lost touch with those important roots; she had little time for social status, and for her faith was not an easy optional extra but a tough discipleship that required concentration, dedication and openness to God at all times.

At the age of sixteen, she went to stay with Augustinian sisters in Avila, and she began to think that she herself was called to join them. But she fell ill and had to return home. Then she once more left home, this time without her father's knowledge, and entered the Carmelite Convent of the Incarnation at Avila, where she took the habit in 1536. She became ill again and had to leave, eventually returning; throughout this time her experiences of God in prayer became more and more vivid and powerful, though they were often followed by periods of lassitude and depression. She is said to have given up private prayer altogether at one stage, something she never forgot. But she managed some kind of recovery. Her spiritual director was

Baltasar Alvarez, a Jesuit who had become a famous writer and theologian and who had the sense to see that Teresa's experiences were authentic. But it was a difficult time for women, and for books about prayer, since there were a number in Spanish that were under the official ban of the Catholic Church.

Teresa's visions led her towards a new way of working out her calling as a nun, which was to found a convent that would be much more austere than the Carmelite form. Eventually, she received permission from Rome and from the Carmelite Order for the founding of such a convent in Avila in 1542. But no sooner was the convent founded than Teresa was sent on a number of errands. She wrote her autobiography, which was completed in June 1562, just before returning to Avila, where in 1565 a new convent was founded, dedicated to St Joseph, to whom Teresa had great devotion. Her nuns asked for guidance about how they should live together in community and how they should pray. *The Way of Perfection* was the result and it was completed the next year. She went on to write more, including her great classic, *The Interior Castle*.

Teresa held on firmly to her belief that the religious life was essential to the Church in all the difficulties of the time, which included religious wars in France and Germany resulting from the Reformation. Between 1567 and 1582, she founded fourteen new reformed Carmelite convents. A strong personality, she clashed with the central authorities of her Order, and in 1571 she was sent back to her old community, the Convent of the Incarnation in Avila. There were no doubt suspicions about her influence for she had befriended the controversial Juan de Yepes, later known as St John of the Cross, who had helped to found the first male reformed Carmelite house three years earlier. At long last in 1580, a proper Reformed Province of the Carmelites was allowed by the Pope. It was known as the 'Discalced' branch, because of the sandals worn by all its members. She was elected Prioress of St Joseph's Convent in 1581, the year before her death.

*          *          *

What, then, of *The Way of Perfection*?[2] Rowan Williams has described it as 'perhaps Teresa's most consciously mischievous book . . . a conversation between Teresa and her sisters carried on before a rather suspicious audience'.[3] As a controversial figure in her own Church, intent on reforming her own religious order, at a time when reforming influences in the Church were suspect, and the relatively new technology of printing was kept for officially approved works only, Teresa had to walk a delicate tightrope. There is a hint of self-mockery when she describes in the Prologue her purpose as 'to write certain things about prayer; they will see how useless I am . . . my intent is to suggest a few remedies for a number of small temptations which come from the devil' (p.1). That is by any stretch of the imagination a more than modest description of the book that ensued. Of its forty-two chapters, the first eighteen are about the religious community life, chapters nineteen to twenty-six are about prayer in general, and the remaining chapters, approximately one half of the book, are about the Lord's Prayer.

She had promised a 'living book' and this is what we find. The style is lively, perceptive, and sometimes sharp. At a time when many women were made to feel that all they were good for was to recite the Lord's Prayer and the Hail Mary, Teresa turns such a prejudice to her advantage by basing her under-standing of the life of prayer in her community around the Lord's Prayer. For example, in chapter twelve, she writes: 'If you are very careful about your prayer, you will soon find yourselves gradually reaching the summit of the mountain without knowing how . . . be very careful about your interior thoughts, especially if they have to do with precedence' (p.50). We are to take care about prayer, not the order in which we sit in the refectory or the chapel. For 'humility is the principal virtue which must be practised by those who pray' (p.68). The life of prayer is not exclusive, it is for everyone: 'remember, the Lord invites us all' (p.85). Teresa is not trying to popularize spiritual gymnastics. She wants to start – and end – with the Lord's Prayer: 'it is always a great thing to base your prayers on prayers which were uttered by the very lips of the Lord' (p.89), for 'it would be a good idea for us to imagine that He has taught this prayer to each one of us individually, and that He is continually expounding to us' (p.103). As she slips into the text of the Lord's Prayer, Teresa reflects on the first petition: 'What son is there in the world who would not try to learn who his father was if he had one as good, and of as great majesty and dominion, as ours?' (p.112). Divine sonship and daughtership again! Having been somewhat bashful herself in describing this work, she cautions her sisters, 'Avoid being bashful with God, as some people are, in the belief that they are being humble' (p.114). This helps rather than hinders the progress in what she calls 'the prayer of recollection'; 'to conquer oneself for one's own good is to make use of the senses in the service of the interior life' (p.122).

In contemplating the meaning of hallowing the name and the coming of the kingdom, Teresa moves from recollection to 'the prayer of quiet', where faith does not lie dormant in any sense, but where at a unique level we are enabled to see more acutely the paradox of our sinfulness and our being loved and redeemed. 'What is it that sends our faith to sleep, so that we cannot realise how certain we are, on the one hand, to be punished, and, on the other, to be rewarded?' (p.124). Words cease to matter, because each petition of the Lord's Prayer can be sipped and pondered: 'speaking is a distress to them: they will spend a whole hour on a single repetition of the Paternoster' (p.128). On the other hand, such times of quiet simply happen, and they are not to be regarded as specific results successfully achieved: 'there is a saying that if we try very hard to grasp all, we lose all' (p.132). That leads Teresa to interpret the doing of the will on earth as in heaven as a self-surrender, a detachment of ourselves, for 'we are nothing and God is infinitely great' (p.139).

\* \* \*

When it comes to daily bread, Teresa concentrates on the

Eucharist, in particular the reception of Holy Communion and the meditation – for an hour – afterwards. Even though she is anxious about Lutherans profaning the Eucharist, she has – as Moltmann has shown – much in common with Luther himself.[4] The cross and the free gift of God's grace are central to what the Eucharist is about; 'everything we gain comes from what we give' (p.140). 'Consider not His love, which, for the sake of fulfilling Thy will and of helping us, would allow Him to submit day by day to being cut to pieces' (p.142). Faithful reception, such a keynote of the devotional manuals of the seventeenth-century Anglican divines, is central for Teresa: 'entreat Him not to fail you but to prepare you to receive Him worthily' (p.145). In a devotional tradition so foreign to the 'after the vision – the task' eucharistic practice of today, she warns us to 'delight to remain with Him; do not lose such an excellent time for talking with Him as the hour after Communion' (p.148). For after Communion, having received the Lord in the sacrament, we are to look into our own souls: 'when you have received the Lord, and are in His very presence, try to shut the bodily eyes and to open the eyes of the soul and to look into your own hearts' (p.150).

For Teresa careful preparation, prayerful reception, and recollected thanksgiving are central to the meaning of the petition for daily bread: 'if we prepare to receive Him, He never fails to give, and He gives in many ways that we cannot under-stand' (p.151). But she also accepts that those who are not called to the religious life will pray that prayer with an earthly meaning: 'those who still live on earth, and must conform to the customs of their state, may also ask for the bread which they need for their own maintenance and for that of their house-holds, as is perfectly just and right, and they may also ask for other things according as they need them' (p.161).

Teresa sees the grace of the sacrament enabling us to forgive others, as we are forgiven, and to recognize our own imper-fections when faced with temptation. She knows some of the temptations of religion: 'I think the devil is anxious for us to believe that we are humble, and if he can, to lead us to distrust

God' (p.170). Moreover one of the temptations of the religious person is scrupulosity: 'Do not be too strict with yourselves, then, for if your spirit begins to quail, it will do great harm to what is good in you and may sometimes lead to scrupulosity, which is a hindrance to progress both in yourselves and in others' (p.180). Teresa ends this wide-ranging treatment of the Lord's Prayer by underlining its superiority over all other forms of vocal prayer: 'If you have learnt how to say the Paternoster well, you will know enough to enable you to save all the other vocal prayers you may have to recite' (p.185). She thus quietly turns the tables on any who would base the life of prayer on more complex forms, which, she would maintain, are essentially *derivative* from what the Lord himself has given us.

*The Way of Perfection* takes us into a different medium, not retreat addresses, or sermons, or baptismal instruction, but an apparently modest treatise for a new movement within a religious order. And yet it is not a book of set rules, nor is it about prescribing the great moments and visions of spiritual experience that Teresa struggled to articulate earlier in her life. Here is a spiritual giant who can see what is really important in prayer and discipleship. She starts with what is needful, a community truly committed to a corporate life, undistracted by notions of status, and ready, almost by virtue of that commitment, to move forward in its life of prayer. This is a life which is individual as well as corporate, not based on elaborate schemes (which were rightly suspect at the time anyway) or specific personal experiences (which are not always helpful to others), but on the words that Jesus himself taught his disciples – which 'He is continually expounding to us' (p.103). These are the sure foundations. After her death she was rightly venerated, and canonized in 1622; and in 1970 she was declared by Pope Paul VI 'a Doctor of the Church', the first woman to receive such recognition in the Roman Catholic Church.

# Dietrich Bonhoeffer: Community Life (1937)

On 9 July 1998 a service was held in Westminster Abbey for the dedication of statues of twentieth-century Christian martyrs, one of which was of Dietrich Bonhoeffer. It was a dramatic occasion, since that century saw more people die for the Christian faith than any of the preceding ones. Among those present in the Abbey as a guest of honour was Eberhard Bethge. He had collaborated closely with Bonhoeffer in the years of the German Church's struggle before and during the Second World War. His was a poignant presence at such an occasion, a reminder to all present of the significant contribution Bonhoeffer's life and teaching had made to many people all over Europe and beyond, a contribution Bethge himself largely made possible in his biography of Bonhoeffer, and in the editions of Bonhoeffer's works that he helped to compile.

Writing from prison towards the end of his life, Bonhoeffer wrote 'Thoughts on a Baptism' a few weeks after the birth of Bethge's son, who was given the name Dietrich and who played a Bach cello solo sonata at the Westminster Abbey service. Here is a short extract from what Dietrich Bonhoeffer wrote for Dietrich Bethge as an infant: 'Our being Christians today will be limited by two things: prayer and righteous action among men. All Christian thinking, speaking, and organising must be born anew out of this prayer and action. By the time you have grown up, the Church's form will have changed greatly. We are not yet out of the melting pot, and any attempt to help the church prematurely to a new expansion of its organisation will merely delay its conversion and clarification.'[1]

These words are vintage Bonhoeffer. They speak from the heart of a man who struggled to find a Christian faith and who in turn found himself caught up in a struggle of universal proportions. There is a coolness of thinking and a warmth of feeling about much that he wrote. But his prose was no self-indulgent existential angst; rather it was the clear thinking and warm feeling of a man who all the time sought to discipline his words and deeds by the Sermon on the Mount, which was a constant theme in his writing and preaching.

Bonhoeffer was born in 1906 in Breslau (from where the family moved to Berlin in 1912), the son of a professor of Psychiatry.[2] Although some of his forebears were Lutheran pastors and theologians, the home in which he grew up was not a churchgoing one. They sang chorales around the piano at festivals, but they were unimpressed by the Berlin churches. Bonhoeffer's older brother, Walter, was killed at the front in the final year of the First World War. As the Weimar Republic settled into its stride in the tragic years following, the Bonhoeffer family held aloof from the voices of the extreme left and right that were making bids for leadership.

Bonhoeffer grew up a tall, blond and sensitive young man. He decided to study theology at university, starting at Tübingen. He was there during Adolf Hitler's dramatically unsuccessful putsch in Munich. In the summer of 1924 he went to Berlin, where the teaching was conventionally Lutheran. There are indications that he was already sensing the inadequacy of popular Lutheranism, which had so strong an emphasis on justification by faith alone through grace that there seemed to Bonhoeffer little left to say about human response. He found himself increasingly attracted to another theologian, from the Reformed tradition, a man called Karl Barth (1886–1968) who taught in the University of Göttingen. Barth was critical of any form of Christianity that became too comfortable and compromising with the culture of the time. In particular, Barth's reaction to the First World War was to look profoundly at what kind of response the Church could make to the destruction of so much of the inherited structures and attitudes with which the men who went to war in 1914 were imbued. The Faculty of Theology in Berlin were not overjoyed at the bright young Bonhoeffer's attraction to the radical voice in Göttingen.

Bonhoeffer was none the less ordained, and his first responsibilities kept taking him abroad, suggesting a restless spirit, not at ease with his Church. He went to Barcelona as assistant pastor to the German congregation there. A year at Union Theological Seminary in New York followed, during which he made a number of important contacts with theologians, and some important friendships resulted. He returned to work in Berlin as a lecturer and pastor and became more and more opposed to the Nazi threat. He signed the famous Barmen Declaration in 1934, which effectively divided the 'Confessing Church' from the 'German Christians', the latter comprising the bulk of German Protestantism, who one way or another were prepared to accommodate the new government. After serving a Lutheran congregation in London, he returned to Germany in 1935 to head an independent seminary for the Confessing Church in Pomerania at Finkenwalde. The intense corporate life at Finkenwalde, involving daily worship and meditation, was much influenced by what he had experienced in England at the Theological Colleges at Kelham and Mirfield. The seminary was closed by the authorities in 1937. Bonhoeffer then went to America on a lecture tour, where he struggled with an invitation to stay, an offer which he refused in order to return to face the emerging crisis back home. He became involved in resistance to Hitler, leading a mysterious life behind the scenes. He was eventually arrested in 1943 and hanged at Flossenbürg on 9 April 1945, only weeks before the Second World War ended.

\*     \*     \*

*The Cost of Discipleship* is the English translation (which

appeared posthumously in 1948) of a book which was first
published during Bonhoeffer's lifetime in 1937 under the
German title, *Nachfolge*.[3] The English title is a paraphrase of
the German, which means 'following after', and is in itself a
tribute to the author's life. The central portion consists of an
exposition of the Sermon on the Mount, on which Bonhoeffer
had preached and meditated frequently. It reads tersely, like a
concise devotional sermon that combines explanation and
application of the original text. There is no doubt that the
experience of life at Finkenwalde – so untypical of Lutheran
theological training then – lay behind it. There were times of
daily prayer, meditation and mutual confession, which is where
the friendship with Bethge blossomed. Such a corporate life can
be read in many of the pages of *The Cost of Discipleship*, which
is in some respects a summary of Bonhoeffer's theology. In a
sermon in Barcelona in July 1928 he remarked that 'sacrifice,
intercession, absolution, those are the wonderful powers of the
Christian community, which are all contained in the word
Love, Love as God has shown it to us, in becoming Christ to
the other person.' For Bonhoeffer there must be no social or
cultural accommodation by the Church to the spirit of the age.
Instead, Christians must be prepared to put their faith into
practice and be enabled in that process by the very tools given
us by Christ.

The Sermon on the Mount is made up of three chapters of
Matthew's Gospel. The central chapter – that which contains
the Lord's Prayer – Bonhoeffer describes as 'the hidden
character of the Christian life', a hiddenness which is none the
less powerfully present. For Bonhoeffer, there is nothing
obvious, easy or natural about the Gospel. 'Jesus teaches his
disciples to pray. What does this mean? It means that prayer is
by no means an obvious or natural activity' (p.145). 'It matters
little what form of prayer we adopt or how many words we use;
what matters is the faith which lays hold on God and touches
the heart of the Father who knew us long before we came to
him' (pp.145–6). Bonhoeffer unashamedly holds on to prayer
as 'the supreme instance of the hidden character of the

Christian life' (p.146). For 'the right way to approach God is to stretch out our hands and ask of One whom we know has the heart of a Father' (p.147). The depth of the crisis facing human beings is offset by the fact that 'our heavenly Father knows our needs' (p.147).

Perhaps Bonhoeffer's most telling statement is the following: 'The Lord's Prayer is not merely the pattern of prayer, it is the way Christians *must* pray' (p.148). Here he shows himself a spiritual heir of Luther, who wrote several works on the Lord's Prayer, and who also made it prominent in Lutheran liturgy. The pastor and the godparents recite it after the reading of the scripture warrant before the Baptism, the pastor lowering his hand on the infant's head. At Holy Communion, it comes immediately before the narrative of the Last Supper. Both these positions give it a stark prominence. For Bonhoeffer, like Luther, 'the Lord's Prayer is the quintessence of prayer' (p.148).

Bonhoeffer expounds each petition with a short pithy paragraph. 'The call of Jesus binds the disciples into a brotherhood' (p.148). That 'brotherhood' surely evoked the Finkenwalde experience, the fatherhood of God actually *constituting* our brotherhood. Of the hallowing of the name Bonhoeffer prays, 'May God protect his holy gospel from being obscured and profaned by false doctrine and unholiness of living and may he ever make known his holy name to the disciples in Jesus Christ' (p.148). The Church is indeed full of false doctrine and unholiness of living, but for Bonhoeffer this means placing that doctrine and that living under the searchlight of the gospel itself. 'Unholiness' is put on a par with 'false doctrines': abstract teaching is not enough. Writing of the coming of the kingdom, he asserts that 'the kingdom of God is still exposed to suffering and strife' (p.148). 'God grant that the kingdom of Jesus Christ may grow in his Church on earth, God hasten the end of the kingdoms of this world, and establish his own kingdom in power and glory' (p.148). Between these lines we can read the struggle that Bonhoeffer and his followers faced in Nazi Germany. But he goes on: 'His followers must also pray that the will of God may prevail more and more in their hearts every day and break down all defiance' (p.149). For him, daily bread is physical provision, and the disciples 'should not be ashamed to pray for their bodily needs' (p.149).

\*     \*     \*

But what of forgiveness? Bonhoeffer is worth quoting in full. 'Every day Christ's followers must acknowledge and bewail their guilt. Living as they do in fellowship with him, they ought to be sinless, but in practice their life is marred daily with all manner of unbelief, sloth in prayer, lack of bodily discipline, self-indulgence of every kind, envy, hatred and ambition. No wonder that they must pray daily for God's forgiveness. But God will only forgive them if they forgive one another with readiness and brotherly affection. Thus they bring all their guilt before God and pray as a body for forgiveness. God forgive not merely *me my* debts, but *us ours*' (pp.149–50).

This paragraph is the heart of Bonhoeffer's exposition of the Lord's Prayer. There is a passion and a directness that bring us to the foot of the cross and humble us. Three times he stresses the 'daily' aspect of not only praying for forgiveness, but of forgiving other people, and of doing so in a fellowship of love and costly discipline. He lists sins in terms of unbelief, sloth in prayer, lack of bodily discipline, self-indulgence, envy, hatred, and ambition. Personal, mutual confession to another person at Finkenwalde can be seen here in a poignant way, particularly if one realises that Bonhoeffer's confession partner was Eberhard Bethge, a man who understood him so well. Forgiveness must not be grudging, it must be done with readiness and affection, and sin is not individual but it is collective, so that disciples need to pray together for each other's forgiveness. It is also worth recalling the Lutheran practice (which Bonhoeffer will have known) of private confession to the pastor, especially before Holy Communion. At the end of the day, Bonhoeffer and Teresa of Avila are not so far apart in context, since they are both writing about religious community.

Bonhoeffer links the prayer for forgiveness with the petitions that follow. 'The disciple is conscious of his weakness, and does not expose himself unnecessarily to temptation in order to test the strength of his faith' but 'the last petition is for deliverance from evil and for the inheritance of the kingdom of heaven' (p.150). The doxology renews 'the disciples' assurance that the Kingdom is God's by their fellowship in Jesus Christ, on whom depends the fulfilment of all their prayers' (p.150).

The Lord's Prayer is central to Bonhoeffer, because it is fundamentally about Christian obedience, a word he uses to draw together the truth of justification by Christ and the reality of discipleship. In the *Prayerbook of the Bible: An Introduction to the Psalms* (1940), the last of his writings published in his lifetime, he saw the Lord's Prayer as an embodiment of the gospel itself, as the Christian embodiment of the Psalter, and as the summation of all prayer. He ends by quoting Luther's preface to the Neuburg Hymn-book of 1545:

Our dear Lord, who has taught and given us the Psalter and the Lord's Prayer to pray, give us also the spirit of prayer, and the grace that we may with joy and sincerity pray with a true faith and without ceasing; for we are in need of it; and thus he commanded and desires from us: to Him the praise and honour and thanksgiving. Amen.[4]

# Gregory of Nyssa: Sermons (370s)

Cappadocia was the name of the province of the Roman Empire which made up the central-east portion of Turkey. The terrain consisted of a rolling plateau, the mountainous parts of which had severe winters. Certain cereals and fruit could be grown, and grazing could be rich; the Persian Kings took many horses, sheep and mules from its pastures and Roman emperors had stud farms for their racehorses there. Cappadocia knew an early Christian presence, for its inhabitants are mentioned in the catalogue of peoples in Acts 2:9.

Between modern day Ankara (Ancyra) and Kayseri (Caesarea) lie the ruins of the ancient small town of Nyssa, where around 371 Gregory was made Bishop of a new diocese.[1] He was a reluctant occupant of episcopal office, for he was pressurized into the post by his dominant elder brother, Basil of Caesarea, who had taught him during his earlier life, and who was reorganizing the ecclesiastical province under his care. The two had a somewhat uneasy relationship. Gregory was present at Basil's death around 379, but Gregory was closer to his sister Macrina, whose life he wrote and at whose funeral he preached.

Gregory was born about 330 and grew up with Christianity with his two siblings. Although he sensed the call to the priesthood his first profession was that of a rhetorician, like Cyprian of Carthage, and he never lost the influence either of his brother's teaching or of the philosophical and legal training that a rhetorician received. At Nyssa Gregory was a fine teacher and preacher, but he was not always firm or adept with money. Like other bishops of the time, he had to deal with the theological controversies concerning the two natures of Christ and the doctrine of the Trinity. In 376, a Synod at Nyssa deposed him because a pro-Arian group, which wanted to emphasize the human character of Christ as against the divine, had taken control. Gregory went into exile but was restored only two years later. He was becoming renowned as a theologian, and in 380 was elected Bishop of Sebaste in the north-east of the province, but he withdrew and returned to Nyssa. A year later, he was prominent at the Council of Constantinople in 381 that defined Christian orthodoxy, and was chosen to preach the funeral sermon for Meletius, Bishop of Antioch, the first president of the Council. Gregory died around the year 394.

Gregory is numbered among the so-called 'Cappadocian Fathers', usually reckoned in third place to Basil of Caesarea (his older brother), and their mutual friend Gregory of Nazianzus. Whilst Basil and the other Gregory have long been venerated, Gregory of Nyssa has been regarded with a tinge of suspicion in the East because of the obvious debt that he owed to Origen, the Alexandrian theologian of the previous century whose writings were often controversial through his love of interpreting scripture from an allegorical point of view. The three Cappadocians were largely responsible for clarifying the Church's understanding of the Trinity in relation to the divinity of the Holy Spirit. The Godhead could not consist of Father and Son, with the Spirit as an appendage. The Spirit had to share fully in the divine nature, and there are signs of this in Gregory's teaching on the Lord's Prayer.

The tradition of the Greek philosopher Plato in early Christian thought led him to the view that there are two ways of knowing God; one through looking at the givens of nature and the universe, the other being the mystical way, by stripping the soul of anything bodily and abandoning all concepts in order to plunge into the divine darkness where the soul knows only by faith; here, the soul can reach forward and explore the nature and love of God. There is a flavour of this, too, in his teaching on the Lord's Prayer. For all Gregory's belief in the perfectibility of the human race, to the point of suggesting that even the devil can one day share in the perfect vision of God, he recognizes the reality of sin and evil, which also gently pervades his teaching on the Lord's Prayer. In one of his writings, he illustrates Christ's conquest of the devil by suggesting that Christ 'was concealed under the veil of a human nature, so that, as with a greedy fish, the hook of divinity might be swallowed along with the bait of flesh'.[2] This fish-hook image he uses in the fifth sermon on the Lord's Prayer, but the other way around, to illustrate the tempting hook of evil.

\* \* \*

Gregory preached five sermons on the Lord's Prayer[3] and in style they are plainer and more practical than his technical theological writings. It is clear that he is preaching to an ordinary congregation, not specifically those preparing for Baptism. We do not know the date, but it is thought that they were written before the Council of Constantinople (381); and because bishops had a strong preaching ministry, we may conclude that they date from the 370s. The sermons explain the nature of prayer and the meaning of the Lord's Prayer with a view to exhorting the congregation towards greater attention to the need for prayer, both public and private, and to understand the meaning of the realities that surround them day by day. The first sermon is about the need and nature of prayer; the second is about the first petition; the third concerns the Name and the kingdom; the fourth is about the doing of the will and prayer for bread; and the last expands the prayer for forgiveness and the prayer against temptation and evil.

The first sermon begins almost abruptly. 'The Divine Word teaches us the science of prayer' (p.21). By that very sentence, Gregory lifts the words of the Lord's Prayer from the level of being no more than words in themselves to a divine command in the here and now so that we can learn what the nature of prayer is. It is the prayer of a fallen creature which is redeemed: 'when I was exiled from Paradise, deprived of the tree of life, and submerged in the gulf of material things, was it not He who brought me back to man's first beatitude?' (p.26). His Christian

Platonism comes across more directly in the contrast he draws between the heaven above in perfection, and earth below, fallen but still perfectible; 'all things depend indeed on the Divine Will, and life here below is ordered from above' (p.32).

The second sermon, on the heavenly Fatherhood, develops these themes further. 'The words seem to me to indicate a deeper meaning for they remind us of the fatherland from which we have fallen and of the noble birthright which we have lost' (p.41). We lost our 'noble birthright' at the Fall and we can regain it through Christ. At the end of this sermon he states that 'we should always look at the beauty of the Father and fashion the beauty of our own soul on His' (p.44), which presumably he would interpret as the kind of 'knowing God' which strips the soul bare of all that is earthly. And, as if to bring home his point, he goes on to remark that 'the Divine is pure from envy and from all stain of passion' (p.44). He uses the theme of keeping apart from evil later in the prayer.

The third sermon, on the hallowing of the Name and of the coming of the kingdom, builds on our capacity to do good. 'Human nature is too weak to achieve anything good and therefore we can obtain nothing of the things for which we are anxious unless the good be accomplished in us by Divine aid. And of all good things the most important for me is that God's Name shall be glorified through my life' (p.48). Gregory refuses to locate the hallowing of the Name in worship alone, and insists on spreading it throughout the whole of life. But how? By the work of the Holy Spirit, fully divine. And here we come to his treatment of the Trinity.

Claiming divine authority for the divinity of the Holy Spirit, he notes that according to *his* text of the New Testament, Luke's version of the Lord's Prayer does not give 'your kingdom come', but 'may thy Holy Spirit come upon us and purify us' (p.52). Here, Gregory quotes it with approval, and he is followed in the next century by another Greek Father, Maximus the Confessor, who also wrote a commentary on the Lord's Prayer. A few late manuscripts of Luke's Gospel do indeed follow such a reading, and while the 'authentic' version is still held to be 'your kingdom come', it is not altogether incompatible with Luke's view of the Holy Spirit in his Gospel, where the word 'Spirit' refers to the work of God more frequently than in Matthew and Mark. This leads Gregory to interpret this part of the Lord's Prayer in a Trinitarian way, which he illustrates in the forgiveness of sins: 'if therefore the Father forgives sins, the Son takes away the sins of the world, and the Holy Spirit cleanses from the stains of sin those in whom He dwells' (p.56).

The fourth sermon deals with the doing of the will and the prayer for daily bread. Purification is the key to the former: 'therefore the prayer teaches us thus to purify our life from evil, that the will of God may rule in us without hindrance, in the same way as it does in the life of heaven' (p.62). And uniquely among the early Christian Fathers, he is unequivocal in his contention that the prayer for bread is about ordinary human sustenance: 'ask for bread because life needs it, and you owe it to the body because of your nature' (p.64). And why? Because the natural needs sustenance in its journey to the supernatural: 'bread is for our use today; the Kingdom belongs to the beatitude for which we hope' (p.70).

\*　　\*　　\*

In the fifth and final sermon, Gregory deals with forgiveness, temptation and evil. These themes have been strong already in these sermons, because human nature is perfectible – but only perfectible if we make progress in the life of faith and use the grace of God and the knowledge of him that are open to us. The truth of human forgiveness is so great for Gregory that it leads him to exaggerate the mutuality inherent in the Gospel passage. First of all, we ourselves are given the ability to judge our sins: 'be yourself your own judge, give yourself the sentence of acquittal' (p.73). We are able ourselves, so it seems, to cancel all the sins that we have committed and leave the court of justice without a stain on our character. But that is because we forgive others, and thereby ask God to imitate us by him forgiving us our sins. In making such a bold claim, he dares to address God in this part of the sermon: 'I have shown great mercy to my neighbour – imitate thy servant's charity, O Lord' (p.74). Such an inversion of agency, placing the human race rather than God in the position of taking the initiative is unique, and only serves to highlight the reality of divine grace and the distance between ourselves and God that is bridged by the work of Christ.

This leaves Gregory to move on to discuss what these sins actually are that we so readily forgive of others and ask to be forgiven ourselves. The contrast between the divine and the human worlds appears again: 'instead of the divine garments we have put on luxuries, and reputation, transitory honours and the quickly passing satisfactions of the flesh, at least as long as we look at the place of distress in which we have been con-demned to sojourn' (p.76). Gregory enumerates the passing things that continue to tempt and attract us, and the reality of the dimensions in which we live on earth. But our life on earth is only temporary, a preparation for the heavenly, whose garments (perhaps an allusion to the baptismal robe) are eternal and they can be seen in the life of grace as lived and expressed by Christ.

Gregory merges the prayer against temptation and for deliverance from evil into one, and safeguards the eternal sovereignty of God by going so far as to *equate* the two peti-tions: 'if a man prays truly to be delivered from evil, he asks that he may be far from temptation' (p.89). Even if he does not resolve the dilemma (we must keep away from the baits of temptation, not face them out), Gregory's is a subtle way of leaving his hearers suitably challenged to take the words of the Lord's Prayer to heart.

# Lancelot Andrewes: Sermons (1611)

In 1611, the Authorised Version of the Bible was published, often referred to as the 'King James Bible'. Its influence on the religious and cultural life of the English-speaking people has been immense. But in the same year, a less well-known book also appeared, a collection of nineteen sermons on prayer and the Lord's Prayer by Lancelot Andrewes. Andrewes had been involved in the translation of the first part of the Old Testament of the Authorised Version, and at the time was Bishop of Ely. It could be a coincidence that he chose to publish these sermons in the same year as the new translation of the Bible. But it could also have been deliberate. For Andrewes' contribution to the theological scene both in his own century and since was primarily as a remarkably original biblical preacher whose inner life of prayer was echoed in what he said from the pulpit, and whose own private devotions often echoed exact words from his published sermons. Correspondences like these between preaching and praying lead us again and again not so much to the *text* of scripture as to its *use*. For Andrewes lived at a time when there were those who wanted to elevate scripture above all else, rather than place it within the praying life of the Church, whether in the public liturgy or in private devotion.

Andrewes was born in 1555 at Barking, the son of a merchant seaman, and he went to the Merchant Taylors' School.[1] He proceeded to Pembroke Hall, Cambridge, where his academic ability was soon identified. Ordained to a fellowship he was made Catechist of the College, which involved giving teaching sermons every week. In 1589 he was appointed vicar of St Giles', Cripplegate, in the City of London, as well as

Master of Pembroke, where his practical ability enabled him to set the college finances on a sure footing. He attracted attention from the Royal Court and preached before Elizabeth I from time to time in the 1590s. In 1601 he was made Dean of Westminster and therefore was involved with the funeral of Queen Elizabeth I and the coronation of King James when he came from Scotland in 1603. There appears to have been a close friendship between the two and Andrewes was soon made a bishop, first of Chichester in 1605, then of Ely in 1609, and finally of Winchester in 1619; he died in 1626. During those years as a bishop he preached before the Royal Court on nearly all the great Christian festivals. After his death an edited collection was published of many of these sermons, ninety-six in all. They are something of set-piece performances, elaborate in construction and full of biblical and patristic quotations. Also after his death his private devotions – the 'Preces Privatae' – were published both in the original Latin, Greek and Hebrew in which Andrewes prayed them, and also in various English translations.

Andrewes has attracted attention across the years from a number of different scholars such as T. S. Eliot, the poet, and Nicholas Lossky, the Russian Orthodox lay theologian. Theologically it is impossible to label him. As a faithful son of the Reformation, he is loyal to the Prayer Book, to the free gift of God's grace, and to the impossibility of limiting God in any way. On the other hand he is a man of tradition, who sees the Church of England in continuity with the Church of the early centuries, hence his delight in quoting the Early Fathers; he would often include Augustine in the West and John Chrysostom in the East in the same sermon, as if to make what might nowadays be described as an ecumenical point.

What of the nineteen sermons on prayer and the Lord's Prayer? They are noticeably different in presentation and length from the 'Ninety-Six' that were collected together after his death. Although published in 1611, they appear to be a course of sermons preached earlier in Andrewes' career, either at Cripplegate or at Cambridge. The style is simpler and they are sometimes presented in such a way as to read more like extended notes than the full version as actually delivered. They do not go in for the sometimes sharp illustrations of the 'Ninety-Six', but they are still vintage Andrewes. The Lord's Prayer must mean everything, and every single option is explored. It is clear, too, that the subject was very dear to Andrewes. There are no fewer than forty direct echoes of these sermons in the 'Preces Privatae', where there is also a full section on the Lord's Prayer.[2]

*   *   *

The first six of these nineteen sermons are introductory and lead into the remaining thirteen.[3] In the first, he insists that 'in our regeneration not only the corruption of our will is healed, but a certain divine spark of fire and zeal of God's spirit is infused into us, by which we are holpen to do those duties of piety, which otherwise naturally we have no power to do' (p.307). The Christian still has an innate capacity towards good, in spite of the Fall. In the third sermon, he refuses to accept the Lord's Prayer as only optional, and holds fast to the need for a set form of prayer given by Jesus: 'whereas He seteth down a form of prayer, He showeth that prayer is necessary; but when unto both He addeth a precept, we may not think any longer it is a matter indifferent but of necessity; a command-ment is a thing obligatory' (p.323). He emphasizes this point further in the fourth sermon: 'we are not only exhorted by religion to use it, but nature itself binds us unto it; for so long as we can devise any help of ourselves, or receive it from any other, so long we lean upon our own staff, but when all help fails, then we fly to prayer as our last refuge' (p.334). Andrewes the pastor of souls knows the importance of prayer sometimes as a final resort. But in the sixth sermon he recognizes human nature before God by pointing to the prayer's structure: 'if a man did make a prayer, he would begin at daily bread; but Christ in this prayer teacheth us "first to seek the kingdom of God"' (p.361). Between these lines we can probably discern the protest of radical Puritans against using the Lord's Prayer at all, against set prayers of any kind, and in favour of extempore prayer at all times.

In the seventh sermon, on Our Father, Andrewes states that 'God can never cease to be "Our Father" though He be ever so much offended, and we cannot cease to be His sons, howsoever wicked we may be; and therefore God doth by an immutable term signify unto us the immutability of His affection' (pp.366f). This draws from him an echo from the 'Preces Privatae' in the following address to God: 'Although, Lord, I have lost the duty of a son, yet Thou hast not lost the affection of a Father' (p.367).[4] The Lord's Prayer is unique, different from all other prayers in that it is a prayer 'of charity', given by the Lord, not 'of nature', and composed by the Church: 'this prayer which our Saviour sets down for us, and all Christians' prayers, are not the prayers of nature, but the prayers of charity' (p.369). But Christian life involves putting this charity into practice: 'there must be an imitation, and we must set ourselves forward to our heavenly country' (p.379). Hence the duty of prayer is not to impress God but to ask for his grace: 'the care that He hath for the sanctifying of His name ariseth from the duty which man oweth unto Him' (p.383).

Andrewes contrasts the limited way in which this world can distinguish the coming kingdom from the heavenly kingdom: 'as before we prayed for the kingdom of glory, so now for this kingdom of grace; for without this we shall never be partakers of that other kingdom' (p.393). 'We pray not so much that God's will may be done, but rather that what God willeth may be our will; for there is one will of God which we may resist, another which we may not resist. For the distinction of God's will, it is either hidden and secret, or revealed and open' (p.397). In that kingdom of grace, we need God's presence walking before us and coming after us: 'as He prevents us with His grace by giving us both a will and a power, so He must still follow us with His grace that we may go forward in doing of his will' (p.403). He here makes the important distinction between what we can resist and what we cannot of God's will, between his eternal good purposes, and the partial glimpses we have, including when we get things wrong. We want to do God's will, and sometimes it is easy to do and at other times it is not; and sometimes it is not obvious, whereas at other times it is.

Andrewes is always conscious of structure. In the next sermon ('in earth as it is in heaven') he remarks that 'this prayer contains two *sicuts* (= as); the one pertains to God, teaching us how to love Him; the other concerns our neighbour, where we pray to be forgiven as we forgive our debtors' (p.406). Like Gregory of Nyssa he believes in an exclusively physical interpretation of daily bread: 'our request to God is for that food which is gotten by honest pains taken in our calling' (p.420); it is something of a surprise that he interprets it in this way, given the fact that so many of his festival sermons in the 'Ninety-six' end by applying the text to the Eucharist.

Coming to the theme of forgiveness, Andrewes remarks that 'we have to pray God for remission . . . because our sins do make a partition between God and us' (p.425). But as a shrewd pastor, he cannot sign up to the view that we can 'forgive and forget' because he knows that the human memory is infinitely more subtle: 'we cannot utterly forget an injury' (p.438). Linking temptation and forgiveness he remarks that 'we are no less to desire of God that He will give us ability to resist sin to come, than to be gracious to us in pardoning our sins already committed' (p.441). And he neatly distinguishes between not being led into temptation and being delivered from evil: 'when we pray that we be not led into temptation, we desire that we do no evil; when we pray that we may be delivered from evil, our desire is that we may suffer no evil' (p.450).

\*   \*   \*

In the eighteenth sermon, Andrewes proceeds to the doxology. This needs some explanation. In the previous century, as has already been pointed out, Calvin had taken the view that the doxology belonged with the rest of the Lord's Prayer, and this had led to its adoption by most Churches of the Reformation.

But in the first Prayer Books, the doxology does not appear. Andrewes, however, *does* include it in his 'Preces Privatae'. In his lifetime, it came to be included in a Prayer Book which King James had compiled for use in Scotland in 1619, probably under Presbyterian pressure. It only entered the English Prayer Book in 1662.

It is therefore no surprise that Andrewes thus explains the doxology in a sermon to a congregation who may not have used it publicly: 'so touching prayer, our Saviour Christ, to shew that it is an indecent thing for any having done his petitions to break off suddenly, or to begin his prayer without any introduction, hath not only made an entrance to His prayer wherein He acknowledged God's goodness, but also addeth a conclusion wherein He confesseth His "Kingdom, Power and Glory"' (p.458). Andrewes' sense of structure brings him to see the need to conclude the prayer in the manner of a doxology (and he alludes to Eastern liturgical practice). Just as the Lord's Prayer itself is not 'a thing indifferent', so is the doxology. He regards it as essential: 'neither is this confession and acknowledgement left to our own choice as a thing indifferent, but we must account of it as of a necessary duty which in no wise be omitted, seeing God enters into covenant that He will hear us and deliver us out of trouble, when we call upon Him' (p.460). Perhaps he helped the process along whereby the doxology was finally added in 1662.[5]

Like others before him, he proceeds to contrast the heavenly kingdom with earthly kingdoms, heavenly power with earthly power, heavenly glory with earthly glory. The kingdom, for whose coming we have prayed near the start of the prayer, is about us: 'we are God's kingdom, and therefore it belongeth to Him to seek our good' (p.462). Yet the kingdom, the power and the glory are God's, and as a preacher who uses many an occasion to bring in the Trinity, he suggests that 'these words, Kingdom, Power, and Glory, being jointly considered, are a representation of the Trinity . . . "the Kingdom" is to be ascribed unto Christ, "Power" to the Holy Ghost, and "Glory" to the Father' (p.463). The three are bound together: 'He hath not only a Kingdom and Power, whereby He was able to defend, but a Glory whereby He can also reward His servants and subjects . . . as there is a mutual bond between the King and his people, so there is between God and us' (p.464). And he goes on to expound the eternal character of that Kingdom and Power and Glory in the words 'for ever and ever'.

The last sermon is on 'Amen'. Andrewes takes care to explain its meaning not only as a sign of assent but as prayer, faith and commitment that it will indeed happen. 'We must not limit God' (p.474) and measure him by our own standards. We must be ready to say 'Amen' not only to the final but to each part: 'our Amen be indivisible, that is, we must say Amen to every petition of the Lord's Prayer; for naturally our corruption is such that we can be content to desire the accomplishment of some of them but not of others' (p.474). Perhaps Andrewes knew of the practice in the old Spanish (Visigothic) liturgy of the priest reciting each petition of the Lord's Prayer on his own, and the congregation responding with their 'Amen' each time. And so the rich range of meanings and applications of this 'prayer of charity' comes to an end.

# Epilogue

'We are bidden to pray'.[1] This is the simple way in which Karl Barth, one of the greatest theologians of the twentieth century, begins his exposition of the Lord's Prayer. Our journey so far has taken us in and out of the New Testament, and round many liturgical traditions, and into some of the most remarkable Christian thinkers. It was inevitable that words so apparently simple and commended for such open-ended use should enter into the vagaries of human experience in the way that they have. There has seldom been a command to pray so variously obeyed, in such different contexts, or with so many probings into meaning, for Jesus never defines, whether in ethnic, national, or religious terms, the community to which this prayer is given.

'In the Lord's Prayer the whole meaning of prayer is summed up.' So wrote Michael Ramsey over sixty years ago. And he immediately went on to say that 'the Lord's Prayer cannot be understood apart from the whole ministry and teaching of Jesus.'[2] The Lord's Prayer is a living text, whose narrative is constantly being written, a narrative made up of the ministry and teaching of Christ as that keeps interacting with our response as obedient disciples as part of the Church Catholic. That living text lives in the *issues* surrounding its origin and use; the *meanings* given to each constituent part; as well as the different *interpreters*, whether they are preaching a sermon, giving a retreat address, preparing baptism candidates, or commenting on community life. The prayer, therefore, lives at the point of tension between what theology calls scripture, tradition and reason; what many will nowadays describe more holistically as their 'experience'; and what David Brown has recently explored as 'tradition and imagination.'[3]

Such use and interpretation has developed through many different cultures, and this process is set to continue – inevitably. The post-Galileo world no longer sees the earth as the centre of the universe, yet the reticence of the Lord's Prayer avoids commitment to an outmoded spatial view of heaven. The third Christian Millennium is bound to bring in new discoveries and new perspectives of all kinds. If one bears in mind the difference between the Anglo-Saxon version of a thousand years ago and the version in use today, it is nothing short of astounding to consider what it will look like in the future, even if this means that future generations may have the chance to learn of its inner strength without relying on its cultural familiarity. Its deep rhythms are set to provide a point of focus, as in previous generations.

The prayer's meaning, however, can never be fully expressed on any one occasion. For example, when Gregory of Nyssa insists that 'daily bread' refers to our material needs, over against a tradition that had interpreted it spiritually or eucharistically, he was right. But so were those other commentators as well. When Lancelot Andrewes describes temptation as we ourselves *committing* evil, and deliverance as we ourselves not *suffering* it, he was perhaps hitting an important nail on the head. But that insight needs to be counterbalanced by the long memory of Christian martyrdom represented by Cyprian's teaching – 'do not suffer us to be led into temptation' – and for which he gave his life. Leonardo Boff, from the perspective of Latin American Liberation Theology, sees the kingdom of God as living out the values of Christ himself among the poor, thus challenging any cosy over-spiritualizing of the Christian faith.

Although for obvious reasons we have only been able to discuss questions of English translation, there have been enough object lessons so far: the words need to be simple, and they need to resonate with a range of meanings, historical and eternal, material as well as spiritual. It is no coincidence that the two most debated parts of the prayer are to do with what are sometimes regarded as humanity's perceived greatest need (food of whatever kind) and greatest fear (the future). It is also no coincidence that the part of the prayer we most often struggle with is forgiveness itself, which it is clear Jesus understood fully from the start. How we interpret these needs, fears and struggles – and the prayer as a whole – has to match up to our understanding of God, who is both involved with – and distant from – the creation; how we both rest in and wrestle with God; how our faith manages at one and the same time to rebel and to accept. There is a fundamental paradox here, and it is about our responsible use of freedom, alongside our capacity for self-surrender.

As far as the use of the prayer is concerned, a number of observations emerge. The prayer should be introduced on every occasion, so enabling everyone to recite the opening words 'Our Father'. It should end with the doxology. This would be in line with Eastern tradition, the Reformation, and the ecumenical consensus of our own time – quite apart from the intrinsic meaning of the doxology, and the way in which kingdom, power and glory refer back to the prayer in different ways. Consideration might also be given to praying in such a way that each petition has its own 'Amen' (like the old Spanish Visigothic rite).

With regard to its position, between the eucharistic prayer and communion, and as part of the conclusion of Morning and Evening Prayer, are arguably the best for the Eucharist and the daily offices. But the old Syrian and Armenian practice of placing it *immediately* after Baptism should be given serious thought. And while the Matthew version has long held sway, there may be occasions when the Lucan text could be used, as something of a stark contrast. We also hope that the tradition of paraphrase writing will continue, to nourish both private and public praying – variety of use can indeed be a sign of health. The Lord's Prayer could be paraphrased into public intercession, as in Calvin's service or for devotional use, as in Charles de Foucauld. Theological writers should be encouraged to keep examining the Lord's Prayer and leave – as they inevitably do – their own marks on their work. But prayer and silence are as closely linked as prayer and words; and we must not forget the tradition of meditating on each part of the Lord's Prayer as described by Teresa of Avila.

*     *     *

Broadly speaking, there are two ways to use the Lord's Prayer: one is to expound it, the other is to pray it, and while each is clearly necessary to the other, they are none the less distinct activities. Our study has drunk deep into the collective memory of the Christian traditions of East and West. This has its limits, for all the variety of authors and rites that we have mentioned. It is appropriate, therefore, that an expositor and a liturgy should have the last word.

Thomas Aquinas was one of the most brilliant theologians of the thirteenth century. It is to him that are attributed the hymns associated with the feast of Corpus Christi, including 'Thee we adore, O hidden Saviour'. In 1273, the year before his death, he preached a course of sermons on the Lord's Prayer and the Apostles' Creed in Naples, where he was then living and teaching. The sermons were for a lay audience, and appended to them is a summary which provides its own grasp of the prayer's shape, biblical background, and practical application, and it is cast in terms of the good that we should desire, a favourite part of his theological framework:

> 'Our Father'. Let it be understood that everything which should be desired is contained in the Lord's Prayer, and everything which should be avoided. Amongst everything which is desirable is that which should most be desired and loved, and this is God: therefore you seek first the glory of God when you say 'Hallowed be your name'. Three things, however, are desired by God in your respect. Firstly, that you should attain to everlasting life, and you ask for this when you say 'Your kingdom come'. Secondly, that you should do the will of God and act justly, and you ask this when you say, 'Your will be done on earth as in heaven.' Thirdly, that you

should have those things necessary for everyday life, and you ask this when you say, 'Give us today our daily bread'. The Lord talks about these three things in Matthew 6:33, with respect to the first when he says 'strive first for the kingdom of God', to the second 'and his righteousness', and to the third 'and all these other things will be given to you.' Those things which are to be avoided, and from which you should flee, are contrary to good.

Moreover the good, which is first to be desired, is fourfold. First is the glory of God, and to this no evil is injurious. Job 35:6,7, 'if you have sinned, what do you accomplish against him? If you are righteous, what do you give to him?' For the glory of God resounds as much when he punishes evil as when he rewards good. The second good is eternal life, to which sin is deleterious since through sin it is lost. Therefore we ask for this to be removed when we say 'Forgive us our sins as we forgive . . .' The third good is justice, and good works, and against these is set temptation, for temptations hold us back from doing good. We ask for these to be taken away when we pray 'And lead us not into temptation.' The fourth good is the good things of life, to which are opposed adversities and tribulations: we seek to be spared these when we ask 'But deliver us from evil'.[4]

The Liturgy of St John Chrysostom is the form of Eucharist most frequently used in churches of the Byzantine rite, which includes Greek and Russian Orthodox, Ukrainian, Melkite, and others. We have already observed John Chrysostom's commitment to the doxology as an integral part of the prayer in the late fourth century. The president's introduction to the prayer has long been attributed to him, and it has been used for centuries. The confident approach to the Father for forgiveness, communion, and the inheritance of the kingdom of heaven speaks for itself:[5]

To you, Master, Lover of humanity,
we entrust our whole life and our hope;

And we entreat, pray and implore you:
count us worthy to partake of your heavenly and awesome
  mysteries
at this sacred and spiritual table,
with a pure conscience, for forgiveness of sins and pardon of
  offences,
for communion of the Holy Spirit,
for inheritance of the Kingdom of Heaven and for boldness
  before you:
not for judgement or condemnation;
and count us worthy, Master,
with boldness and without condemnation
to dare to call upon you, the God of heaven, as Father, and to
  say:

> Our Father in heaven,
> hallowed be your name,
> your kingdom come,
> your will be done,
> on earth as in heaven.
> Give us today our daily bread.
> Forgive us our sins
> as we forgive those who sin against us.
> Lead us not into temptation
> but deliver us from evil.
> For the kingdom, the power,
> and the glory are yours
> now and for ever.
> Amen.

# Appendix

# A Lord's Prayer Hymn and Its Story

Hymn for the Bishop of Portsmouth's Lord's Prayer
Deanery Tour

Tune: Song 34 – 'Forth in thy name'

> Father of Jesus hear us all;
> We lift our earth-bound eyes to you.
> To heavenly life our hearts recall;
> Our faithful Father, fond and true.
>
> Holy, surpassing every name,
> The only God, above all stain;
> In prophet, priest and Son you came:
> Incomprehensible remain.
>
> Reign as our God, rule as our King,
> In all the world your justice bring;
> So wars shall cease, the poor shall feast,
> Joy come to greatest and to least.
>
> Earth yield to heaven, God's will be done
> In each of us as in the Son.
> Dying to self with Christ we rise,
> Drawing all heaven beneath the skies.
>
> Yet, in our human need, we pray
> Your hungry people shall be fed,
> And holy food our Lord convey:
> Give us this day our daily bread.

Daily we sin, O daily pour
Your cleansing grace for us to live.
Though human good was yours before,
Imitate us as we forgive.

Keep us from evil's tempting look,
The pleasing powers which lie in wait,
Lest we take in the deadly hook
All for the greedy, gleaming bait.

Now in the Son the kingdom come,
And in the Spirit power see,
And in the Father glory be,
One God though all eternity.

IAN JAGGER
*October 1999*


## Ian Jagger's Accompanying Letter

11 October 1999

Dear Kenneth,

Here is the hymn for the Lord's Prayer tour. I enjoyed reading the extracts you gave me and hope I have picked out useful things.

In the opening verse I followed Underhill's reference to the '*secret, utterly obedient conversation of Jesus with His Father*', seeing our praying arising out of that example of '*homely confidence*' (the '*awestruck worship*' comes in the next verse), but spreading to 'all' ('*the praying soul accepts once for all its true status as a member of the whole family of man. Our Father. It can never again enter into prayer as a ring-fenced individual*'. '*This refusal of private advantage is the very condition of Christian prayer.*' Because man is a '*borderland creature*' we come to prayer from an 'earth-bound' perspective to be restored to a 'life' whose source is above ('*how far beyond those orderly acts of worship and petition was that living inter-course with the living Father . . .).* The image of 'recalling hearts' leads me straight to the return of the prodigal son to his 'faithful' father who is 'fond' in that slightly indulgent, utterly committed way which is balanced by the double meaning of 'true' – loyal and upright.

In the second verse I focused on F. D. Maurice's *'How can we hallow the name of God? . . . We cannot hallow it; we cannot keep it from contact with our folly, baseness, corruption; the world cannot keep it; the Church cannot. But Thou canst.'* So the fourth line is a reverent plea. In recognizing this I also wanted to acknowledge that God *has* disclosed himself in prophet (word) and priest (sacrifice) and Son but the mystery of his holiness remains intact as the measure and guarantee of the created order. (*'Superstition . . . mixes Him with His creatures.'*) And I had fun doing a Wesley with a six-syllable word.

I enjoyed Leonardo Boff and used *'To believe in the Kingdom of God is to believe in a final and happy meaning for history . . . How will the kingdom of God come? For the Christian faith there is an infallible criterion that signals the arrival of the kingdom: when the poor are evangelized – that is, when justice begins to reach the poor, the dispossessed, and the oppressed.'*

Verse four begins with Cyprian's comment at the end of chapter sixteen *'the earthly should yield to the heavenly, the spiritual and divine should prevail'* and ends with a sense of drawing down all the heavenly realm and order of things and spreading it out *beneath* the heavens, in the earthly realm, so that divine does, indeed, prevail.

I had some trouble with Teresa's angle since most com-mentators agree that 'daily bread' refers to physical human needs, but she is inspiring in her motherly time-capsule. In this verse I needed to register the prayer's move to a very earthly request (hence 'Yet') but, somehow, gather both meanings into the petition about daily bread.

When it comes to the verse about sin I included Bonhoeffer's emphasis on collective and not only personal guilt, but I also strayed over to Gregory of Nyssa in two ways. First, his comments about imitating the divine characteristics and then, second, and with a consequent boldness, that we may say to God, '*Imitate Thy servant, O Lord, though he be only a poor beggar and thou art the King of the universe*'. So I try to say that any goodness we have comes from God anyway, but in the light of that we, as in the original text, may be bold to say to God 'Imitate us'. A sobering challenge. In the earlier reference to grace ('for us to live') I wanted to hint at several possibilities: grace poured on us like baptismal water, grace poured around us in all creation like the harvest of plenty, but also that it is only by grace that we live at all, and grace is there for us to live in, like the air we breathe and the sun's light, a condition of life. The openness of the wording allows those possible understandings of grace though it can never suggest them all.

In the verse about temptation I really wanted to use Gregory's image of the baited hook and I had to work very hard to introduce it in a way that a singing congregation would be able to absorb. I don't know how successful it has been.

Finally, in the doxology, I used Andrewes' Trinitarian reference and ended with eternity.

With the rhyme scheme I decided to use *a.b.a.b.* for the 'earthly' verses and the more balanced couplets for the 'heavenly' ones, with a transition in verse two. In the final verse there is an internal rhyme in the first line and then a concluding (Trinitarian?) triplet.

I hope it will be useful as another element in the deanery tour.

With every good wish,

as ever,

Ian

# Notes

## Part 1 – Issues

### Chapter 1

1. *On Prayer* 18.3; see John O'Meara (tr.), *Origen: Exhortation to Martyrdom* (Ancient Christian Writers 19) (London: Longmans, 1954) p.66.
2. Taken and adapted from J. L. Houlden, 'The Lord's Prayer', in *The Anchor Bible Dictionary* (London: Doubleday, 1992) Vol. IV, p.357 (for whole article, see pp.356–62).
3. The literature on this question is extensive. See, in particular, Ernst Lohmeyer, *The Lord's Prayer* (London: Collins, 1965), and Jean Carmignac, *Recherches sur le 'Notre Père'* (Paris: Letouzey & Ané, 1969). Both these are seminal works, and the latter has an extensive bibliography. See also Graham M. Stanton, *A Gospel for a New People: Studies in Matthew* (Edinburgh: T. & T. Clark, 1992), p.39; I am indebted to Martin Kitchen for drawing my attention to this.
4. F. E. Brightman (ed.), *The Preces Privatae of Lancelot Andrewes* (London: Methuen, 1903) p.285 (see also pp.281–7 for his other material on the Lord's Prayer).

### Chapter 2

1. See Stanton, *A Gospel for a New People*, pp. 285ff, on the Sermon on the Mount.
2. *RB* 20.3–4; see Timothy Fry (ed.), *The Rule of St Benedict in Latin and English with Notes* (Collegeville: Liturgical Press, 1981) pp.216–17.
3. See C. F. Evans, *St. Luke* (London: SCM, 1990) pp.441–80 (esp. pp.474ff on The Lord's Prayer).
4. See, for example, Kenneth Stevenson, *Handing On: Borderlands of Worship and Tradition* (London: Darton, Longman and Todd, 1996) pp.33ff.

## Chapter 3

1. Edwin Muir, *An Autobiography* (London: Methuen, 1964) p.246; I am indebted to Alan Wilkinson for drawing my attention to this.
2. See Kenneth Stevenson, *The Mystery of Baptism in the Anglican Tradition* (Norwich: Canterbury Press, 1998).
3. Caesarius of Arles, 'Sermon' 157 (Exposition of The Lord's Prayer); text in G. Morin (ed.), *Sancti Caesarii Arelatensis Sermones* (Corpus Christianorum Scriptorum Latinorum CIV Caesari Arelatensis Opera, pars I, II) (Turnholti: Brepols, 1953) pp.602–4.
4. Texts in *The Rites of the Catholic Church* (New York: Pueblo, 1976) pp.87ff.
5. This was once attributed to Ildefonsus of Toledo, who flourished in the seventh century; see *Liber de Cognitione Baptismi*, cap LXXXIII, text in *PL* 96.166–7.
6. See Pierre-Marie Gy, 'Liturgie et piété populaire dans le moyen âge postcarolingien', *Nordisk Kollokvium IV i Latinsk Liturgiforskning 15–17 juni 1978 på Lysebu Oslo* (Oslo: Institutt for Kirkehistorie, 1978) p.48 (for whole paper see pp 46–52).
7. See Walter J. Ong, *Orality and Literacy: The Technologizing of the Word* (London: Methuen, 1982).
8. See, for example, *Luther's Works*, Vol. 21 (St Louis: Concordia, 1956) pp.141–8 (Sermon on The Mount, quotation, p.141); Vol. 42 (Philadelphia: Fortress, 1969) pp.15–81 (Exposition of the Lord's Prayer for Simple Laymen); Vol. 43 (Philadelphia: Fortress, 1968) pp.29–38 (Personal Prayer Book), pp.194–200 (A Simple Way to Pray); Vol. 53 (Philadelphia: Fortress, 1965) pp.295–8 ('Vater Unser').

## Chapter 4

1. See Paul F. Bradshaw, *Daily Prayer in the Early Church* (Alcuin Club collections 63) (London: SPCK, 1981) pp.26ff.
2. See Robert F. Taft, 'The Lord's Prayer in the Eucharist: When and Why?', in *Ecclesia Orans* 14 (1997) pp.137–55. See also Ingemar Furberg, *Das Pater Noster in der Messe* (Bibliotheca Theologiae Practicae 21) (Lund: Gleerups, 1968).
3. Text in Marius Férotin (ed.), *Le Liber Mozarabicus Sacramentorum et les Manuscrits Mozarabes* (Paris: Firmin-Didot, 1912) Col.251.
4. *Oeuvres de Saint François de Sales: Edition Complète* Vol. XXVI (Annecy: Monastère de la Visitation, 1932) p.403 (for whole paraphrase, see pp.377–419).
5. See *The Devotions of Archbishop Laud* (Oxford: Parker, 1864) pp.1–5 (the paraphrase comes first in the entire collection).

## Chapter 5

1. Birger Gerhardsson, *The Shema in the New Testament. Deut. 6:4–5 in Significant Passages* (Lund: Nova Press, 1996).
2. Text in *The Christian Year: Collects and Post-Communion Prayers for Sundays and Festivals* (London: Church House Publishing, 1997) p.48.
3. See Reginald Heber (ed.), *The Whole Works of Jeremy Taylor* Vol.III (London: Rivingtons, 1828) pp.75, 79.

## Chapter 6

1. Tertullian, *De Oratione* 1: text in Alexander Roberts and James Donaldson (eds.), *The Ante-Nicene Fathers* Vol.III (Edinburgh: T.& T. Clark, 1993) p.681.
2. See Houlden, *op.cit.* On Mark, see the theory of M. D. Goulder, 'The Composition of the Lord's Prayer', *Journal of Theological Studies* 14 (1963) pp.32–45; on John 21, see Raymond E. Brown, *The Gospel According to John XIII–XXI* (The Anchor Bible) (New York: Doubleday, 1970) pp.739ff.
3. Austin Farrer, *Love Almighty and Ills Unlimited* (London: Collins, 1962) p.188.

## Chapter 7

1. John Calvin, *Institutes of the Christian Religion* Vol III Ch.20, 31, 34.
2. Ian Breward (ed.), *The Westminster Directory* (Grove Liturgical Study 21) (Bramcote: Grove Books, 1980) p.18.
3. Thomas Watson, *The Lord's Prayer* (Banner of Truth) (Avon: The Bath Press, 1993) p.1.
4. See Jan Michael Joncas, 'A Skein of Sacred Sevens: Hugh of Amiens on Orders and Ordination', in Lizette Larson-Miller (ed.), *Medieval Liturgy: A Book of Essays* (New York: Garland Publishing, 1997) pp.85–120.
5. *The Sermons of Hugh Latimer* (Parker Society) (Cambridge: University Press, 1844) p.326.
6. Richard Hooker, *Laws of Ecclesiastical Polity* V xxxv.3.

## Chapter 8

1. See George Steiner, *After Babel* (Oxford: University Press, 1992) pp.296–413.
2. *The Works of John Wesley: Sermons I* (Nashville: Abingdon, 1984) p.573 (whole sermon, pp.572–91).

3. Text in C. K. Barrett (ed.), *The New Testament Background: Selected Documents* (London: SPCK, 1987) p.206; I am indebted to Andrew Tremlett for much assistance here. On the origins and development of the *Kaddish*, see Ismar Elbogen, *Jewish Liturgy: A Comprehensive History* (English translation and updated by R. P. Schiendlin) (Philadelphia: Jewish Publication Society, 1993) pp.80–4; I am grateful to Edward Kessler for drawing my attention to this.

4. See Robert Aron, 'Les origines juives du pater', *La Maison-Dieu* 85 (1966) pp.36–85.

5. Charles Gore, *The Sermon on the Mount: A Practical Exposition* (London: Murray, 1910) p.141.

6. *Expositions and Notes by William Tyndale* (Parker Society) (Cambridge: University Press, 1849) p.81.

7. *The Works of William Beveridge* Vol.8 (Library of Anglo-Catholic Theology) (Oxford: Parker, 1846) p.104.

8. *An Exposition of The Lord's Prayer* (London: Legatt, 1636) p.145.

## Part Two – Meanings

### Chapter 9

1. See Joachim Jeremias, *The Prayers of Jesus* (Studies in Biblical Theology) (London: SCM Press, 1967); and James Barr, 'Abbā isn't "Daddy"', *Journal of Theological Studies* 39.1 (April, 1988) pp.28–47. The literature here is prodigious. I have been helped greatly by two unpublished essays by Benedict Green on the Lord's Prayer in Matthew and in Luke. See also D.C. Parker, *The Living Text of the Gospels* (Cambridge: University Press, 1997) pp.49–74, for a treatment of the Lord's Prayer as an evolving text, affected by traditions of interpretation and translation.

2. See *Common Worship: Services and Prayers for the Church of England – Holy Communion* (London: Church House Publishing, 2000) p.53.

3. William West, *The Nature, Design, Tendency and Importance of Prayer: Illustrated in Seven Practical Dissertations on the Lord's Prayer* (London: Griffiths, 1758) p.7.

4. *Cardinalis S. Bonaventurae Opera Omnia* 10 (Paris: Vives, 1867) 'De Oratione Dominica', p.207 (whole discourse pp.207–10).

5. John Sweet, *Revelation* (London: SCM, 1990) p.115.

6. *The Catechism of Thomas Becon* (Parker Society) (Cambridge: University Press, 1844) p.145.

## Chapter 10

1. See Lohmeyer, *Lord's Prayer* p.71.
2. See Robert F. Taft, 'Holy Things for the Saints: The Ancient Call to Communion and Its Response', in Gerard Austin (ed.), *Fountain of Life: In Memory of Niels K. Rasmussen* (Washington: Pastoral Press, 1991) pp.87–102.
3. *The Scottish Book of Common Prayer* (1929) (Edinburgh: Cambridge University Press, 1929) pp.338f. and 345.
4. William Barclay, *The Lord's Prayer* (Berkhamsted: Arthur James, 1998) pp.36f.
5. Bryan Spinks, *The Sanctus in the Eucharistic Prayer* (Cambridge: University Press, 1991) p.206.
6. 'Expositio Orationis Dominicae', *PL* 178.612–13 (whole text Coll. 611–18).

## Chapter 11

1. See, for example, Jonathan Glover, *Humanity: A Moral History of the Twentieth Century* (London: Jonathan Cape, 1999).
2. The balanced view of 'now/not yet' eschatology is inspired by Joachim Jeremias, *New Testament Theology* Vol.1 (London: SCM, 1971), though I do not follow Jeremias' interpretation of Abbā.
3. Oscar Cullmann, *Prayer in the New Testament* (London: SCM, 1995) pp.45–7.
4. Lohmeyer, *Lord's Prayer* p.105.
5. Geoffrey Wainwright, *Eucharist and Eschatology* (London: Epworth, 1971) p.153.
6. *Maximus the Confessor: Selected Writings* (New York: Paulist Press, 1985) p.108.

## Chapter 12

1. Peter Baelz, *Prayer and Providence* (London: SCM, 1968) p.101.
2. *The Whole Works of Robert Leighton* V (London: Longmans, 1870) pp.277–9.
3. Michael Ramsey, *Jesus and the Living Past* (Oxford: University Press, 1980) p.77.
4. Lesslie Newbigin, *The Open Secret* (London: SPCK, 1978) p.121.
5. *A Collection of Meditations and Devotions in Three Parts* (London, 1717) p.127.

## Chapter 13

1. See for example, Kenneth Stevenson, *Eucharist and Offering* (New York: Pueblo, 1986) p.236.
2. See Carmignac, *Recherches* pp.118–221.
3. Origen, *On Prayer* 27.7, p.96.
4. Andrew McGowan, *Ascetic Eucharists: Food and Drink in Early Christian Ritual Meals* (Oxford: Clarendon Press, 1999).
5. See Robert F. Taft, 'Frequency of the Eucharist throughout History', in *Beyond East and West: Problems in Liturgical Understanding* (Washington: Pastoral Press, 1984) pp.61–80.
6. Quoted in Michael Counsell (ed.), *2000 Years of Prayer* (Norwich: Canterbury Press, 1999) p.411.

## Chapter 14

1. The classic treatment of memory is Augustine, *Confessions* X; see Henry Chadwick (tr.) *Saint Augustine: Confessions* (Oxford: University Press, 1991) pp.179–220; see also Stevenson, *Handing On* pp.17–32.
2. Rowan Williams, *Lost Icons: Reflections on Cultural Bereavement* (Edinburgh: T. & T. Clark, 2000) pp.109, 111.
3. Lohmeyer, *Lord's Prayer* p.176.
4. Peter Selby, *Grace and Mortgage: The Language of Faith and the Debt of the World* (London: Darton, Longman, and Todd, 1997) p.135.
5. *Common Worship: Holy Communion*, p.21.
6. Cullmann, *Prayer in the New Testament*, p.57.
7. Augustine, *Sermon* 56.12; probably preached during the week before Easter, 410–12; see Edmond Hill (tr.) *The Works of Saint Augustine: Sermons* III (New York: New City Press, 1999) p.97.
8. *RB* 13:12–13; see *The Rule of St Benedict*, pp.208–9.

## Chapter 15

1. John Calvin, *Institutes* Vol.III 20.46.
2. See *Praying Together* (Norwich: Canterbury Press, 1988), pp.1–4: the English Liturgical Language Consultation (ELLC) here argues for 'save us from the time of trial', which was debated at the Church of England General Synod in November 1999, where the traditional and less precise translation, 'deliver us not into temptation', was retained.
3. See, in particular, discussions by Carmignac, *Recherches* pp.236–319, Lohmeyer, *The Lord's Prayer* pp.191–229, and Cullmann, *Prayer in the New Testment* pp. 58–67.

4. See C. F. D. Moule, 'An Unsolved Problem in the Temptation Clause in the Lord's Prayer', in *Forgiveness and Reconciliation: Biblical and Theological Essays* (London: SPCK, 1998) pp.190–204.

5. G. G. Willis, 'The Lord's Prayer in Irish Gospel Manuscripts', in *Studia Evangelica* III (Texte und Untersuchungen 88) (Berlin: Akademie-verlag, 1964) pp.282–8.

6. James Walsh (tr.), *The Revelations of Divine Love of Julian of Norwich* (London: Burns & Oates, 1961) p.188 (Ch.68).

7. Barclay, *The Lord's Prayer* pp.107ff.

8. See, for example, F. W. Dillistone, *The Christian Understanding of Atonement* (London: SCM, 1968,1984).

9. *The Works of Thomas Secker* IV (London, 1804) p.288.

10. Tom Wright, *The Lord and His Prayer* (London: SPCK, 1996) p.76.

## Chapter 16

1. See in particular, Carmignac, *Recherches* pp.320–33.

2. John Chrysostom, *Sermon on the Mount*, Homily 19.10; text in Philip Schaff (ed.), *A Select Library of the Nicene and Post-Nicene Fathers*, X (Edinburgh: T. & T. Clark, 1991) p.137. See also Frans Van De Paverd, *Zur Geschichte der Messliturgie in Antiocheia und Konstantinopel gegen Ende des Vierter Jahrtausends: Analyse der Quellen bei Johannes Crysostomos* (Orientalia Christiana Analecta 187) (Roma: Pontificium Institutum Orientalium Studiorum, 1970) pp.371–4.

3. Calvin, *Institutes* Vol.III Ch.20.47.

4. C. F. Evans, *The Lord's Prayer* (London: SCM, 1997) p.88.

5. Stephen Sykes, *Unashamed Anglicanism* (London: Darton, Longman & Todd, 1995) p.308.

6. Mary Hobbs (ed.), *The Sermons of Henry King (1592–1669), Bishop of Chichester* (Cranbury, N.J.: Associated University Presses, 1997) p.218.

## Part 3 – Interpreters

### Chapter 17

1. Among the studies of Evelyn Underhill, particularly useful are Margaret Cropper, *Evelyn Underhill* (London: Longmans, 1958); and Christopher J. R. Armstrong, *Evelyn Underhill (1875–1941): Introduction to her Life and Writings* (London: Mowbrays, 1975).

2. Evelyn Underhill, *Abba: Meditations based on the Lord's Prayer* (London: Longmans, 1940): page references in the text to this edition.

## Chapter 18

1. Among the many studies of Maurice are, Alec Vidler, *The Theology of F. D. Maurice* (London: SCM, 1948); and Arthur Michael Ramsey, *F. D. Maurice and the Conflicts of Modern Theology* (Cambridge: University Press, 1951). See also J. N. Morris, 'A "fluffy-minded Prayer Book fundamentalist?" F. D. Maurice and the Anglican Liturgy', in R. N. Swanson (ed.), *Continuity and Change in Christian Worship* (Studies in Church History 35) (Woodbridge: Boydell and Brewer, 1999) pp.345–60.
2. F. D. Maurice, *The Lord's Prayer: Nine Sermons Preached in the Chapel of Lincoln's Inn* (Cambridge: Macmillan, 1861): page references in the text to this edition. I am indebted to William Norman, Preacher of Lincoln's Inn, for information about the Chapel.
3. F. D. Maurice, *The Kingdom of Christ* II (London: Rivingtons, 1842) pp.43–51 (on the Lord's Prayer), and pp.537f. (passage quoted).
4. F. D. Maurice, *The Prayer Book: Nineteen Sermons Preached in the Chapel of Lincoln's Inn* (London: Macmillan, 1880) p.54.
5. *ibid*, p.55.

## Chapter 19

1. Leonardo Boff, *The Lord's Prayer: The Prayer of Integral Liberation* (Maryknoll: Orbis, 1983) English Translation of *O pai-nosso: a oração da libertação integral* (Petropolis: Vozes, 1979) pp.53f; page references in the text to English edition.
2. Leonardo Boff, *Saint Francis: A Model for Human Liberation* (London: SCM, 1982) p.143; I am grateful to Ann Leonard for drawing my attention to this and the following work.
3. Leonardo Boff, *Trinity and Society* (London: Burns & Oates, 1988) pp.178, 191.

## Chapter 20

1. On Cyprian, see Peter Hinchliff, *Cyprian of Carthage and the Unity of the Christian Church* (London: Chapman, 1974).
2. See above, Ch.6. n.1.
3. T. Herbert Bindley (tr.), *Saint Cyprian on The Lord's Prayer* (London: SPCK, 1904); page references in the text to this edition. For a discussion of early commentaries on the Lord's Prayer in general, see Agnes Cunningham, *Prayer: Personal and Liturgical* (Message of the Fathers of the Church 16) (Wilmington: Glazier, 1985) pp.45–65.
4. There has been a tendency to exaggerate Cyprian's eucharistic theology, underplaying the context of martyrdom and human sacrifice; for

a more balanced view, see J. Laurance, 'Le président de l'Eucharistie selon Cyprien de Carthage: un nouvel examen', *La Maison-Dieu* 154 (1983) pp.151–65.

## Chapter 21

1. See in particular Rowan Williams, *Teresa of Avila* (London: Chapman, 1991).
2. E. Allison Peers (tr.), *Way of Perfection: Saint Teresa of Avila* (London: Sheed & Ward, 1999); page references in the text to this edition.
3. Rowan Williams, *Teresa of Avila*, pp.78f.
4. See Jürgen Moltmann, 'Teresa of Avila and Martin Luther: The Turn to the Mysticism of the Cross', *Studies in Religion/Sciences Religieuses*, 13 (1984) pp.265–78; (quoted in Williams, *Teresa of Avila*, p.107 n.14).

## Chapter 22

1. Eberhard Bethge (ed.), *Dietrich Bonhoeffer: Letters and Papers from Prison* (enlarged edition) (London: SCM, 1971) p.300.
2. Among the studies of Bonhoeffer are the following: Mary Bosanquet, *The Life and Death of Dietrich Bonhoeffer* (London: Hodder & Stoughton, 1968); and Eberhard Bethge, *Dietrich Bonhoeffer, Theologian, Christian, Contemporary* (London: Collins, 1977). See also David F. Ford, *Self and Salvation: Being Transformed* (Cambridge: University Press, 1999) pp.243–65. I am indebted to David Ford for important insights on Bonhoeffer.
3. Dietrich Bonhoeffer, *The Cost of Discipleship* (complete edition) (London: SCM, 1959); page references in the text to this edition. There seems to be one minor slip of translation: 'the Lord's Prayer is not merely the pattern prayer', p.148, which surely should read, 'the pattern *of* prayer', corresponding with 'Das Vater unser ist nicht ein Beispiel für das Gebet der Jüngern' in the original German.
4. Taken from the original German, in E. Bethge and others (eds.), *Gesammelte Werke* 5 (Munich: Chr. Kaiserverlag, 1987) p.569; earlier he states of the Lord's Prayer, 'In ihm ist alles Beten enthalten' (p.547).

## Chapter 23

1. See Anthony Meredith, *Gregory of Nyssa* (London: Routledge, 1998).
2. *Catechetical Oration* 24, in Henry Bettenson (ed. and tr.), *The Later*

*Christian Fathers* (London: Oxford University Press, 1970) p.142.
3. Hilda C. Graef (tr.), *Saint Gregory of Nyssa: The Lord's Prayer, the Beatitudes* (New York: Newman Press, 1954); page references in the text to this edition.
4. *ibid.*, p.187 (n.69).

## Chapter 24

1. Among the various studies of Lancelot Andrewes, the most important is Nicholas Lossky, *Lancelot Andrewes The Preacher* (1555–1626): *The Origins of the Mystical Theology of the Church of England* (Oxford: Clarendon Press, 1991); see also T. S. Eliot, *For Lancelot Andrewes: Essays on Style and Order* (London: Faber, 1928) pp.11–26. See also Kenneth Stevenson, 'Lancelot Andrewes at Holyrood: The 1617 Whitsun Sermon in Perspective', *Scottish Journal of Theology* 54.4 (1999) pp.455–75 (pp.473, nn.33–6 for bibliography). Lossky's study concentrates on the 'Ninety-Six' Court Sermons, but the earlier sermons, including those on the Lord's Prayer, deserve a proper study in their own right.
2. See Brightman, *The Preces Privatae*, where there are around forty allusions to the Sermons on Prayer.
3. See *The Sermons of Lancelot Andrews* Vol.5 (Library of Anglo-Catholic Theology) (Oxford: Parker, 1854); page references in the text to this edition.
4. Cf. 'Though I have lost the ingenuity of a son, Thou hast not lost the affection of a Father', Brightman, *Preces Privatae* p.146.25f.
5. Both William Laud (in his *Devotions*, pp.4f.) and John Cosin (in John Cosin, *A Collection of Private Devotions*, edited by Peter Stanwood and Daniel O'Connor (Oxford: Clarendon, 1967) p.39), also include the doxology in their own use of the Lord's Prayer. These were, of course, for private use, but Cosin's work was published in 1627 for a wider public, and was not uncontroversial in Puritan quarters, though his addition of the doxology will have been welcome to those Puritans who were not opposed to the use of the Lord's Prayer in principle. John Bradford, the Marian martyr (c.1510–55), included it in his treatment, see *The Writings of John Bradford* (Parker Society) (Cambridge: University Press, 1848) pp.138–9.

## Epilogue

1. Karl Barth, *Prayer and Preaching* (London: SCM, 1964) p.24.
2. Arthur Michael Ramsey, *The Gospel and the Catholic Church* (London: Longmans, 1936) p.86.

3. David Brown, *Tradition and Imagination: Revelation and Change* (Oxford: University Press, 1999).

4. P. Mandonnet (ed.), *Thomae Aquinatis Opuscula Omnia* IV (Paris: Lethielleux, 1927) p.41. I am indebted to Gavin Kirk for supplying an English translation.

5. *The Divine Liturgy of Our Father Among the Saints: John Chrysostom* (Oxford: University Press, 1995) pp.38–40.

# Index